O ACOMPANHAMENTO

CHARLES R. HARPER

O ACOMPANHAMENTO

ECUMENICAL ACTION FOR HUMAN RIGHTS IN LATIN AMERICA 1970 – 1990

WCC Publications

Cover design: Claude Dominique Béguin

ISBN 2-8254-1479-4

© 2006 WCC Publications
World Council of Churches
150 route de Ferney, P.O.Box 2100
1211 Geneva 2, Switzerland
Website: http://www.wcc-coe.org

Printed in France

This book is dedicated to the relatives
of victims of enforced disappearance in Latin America,
whose persistent and courageous efforts
to restore the identity and presence of their loved ones,
and to require justice,
illuminate the paths of human history.

Acknowledgements

The author expresses his profound gratitude to
that small group of committed friends of the
ecumenical human rights movement in Latin
America which met informally and regularly
to advise and plan together the actions of
WCC's Human Rights Resources Office for
Latin America during the 1970s and 1980s,
and in particular the late Jaime Wright,
Claudio González, Elsie Monje, Carlos
Sanchez, Aldo Etchegoyen, Alieda
Verhoeven, Rolando Villena and José Burneo.
He was greatly encouraged to write this record
by the late Henry Okullo, Jan Love, Gerson
Meyer, Bill Wipfler, Geneviève Jacques, José
Zalaquett, and Trond Bakkevig, and thanks
both Theo Buss and Dwain Epps for their keen
and helpful observations during its drafting.

Table of Contents

Preface

Two or three years ago I was waiting to board a plane at Ezeiza airport, and, when I went up to a newspaper stand, the young woman at the stand, seeing the Coptic cross I was wearing, asked me, "Are you a priest or a pastor?" When I answered "Yes", she continued, "Were you living in Argentina during the military dictatorship? I belong to the generation that did not experience it and so I have many questions. I would like to know what your experiences were and what you think about it, since I feel I can trust you as a religious person."

In a few minutes' time, two or three had joined us and were listening attentively to what I was saying, including a policeman who happened to be passing and was attracted by the subject...

Between 29 July and 8 August 1985, exactly twenty years ago, the Central Committee of the World Council of Churches was to meet in Buenos Aires and, as the active bishop of my church, it was my task to chair the organizing committee for it. We wondered whether we should have an evening devoted to recalling those days of horror and bloodshed during the military regime, or should we remain completely silent on the subject? Some bishops thought that we should not speak about it, because that would in essence be entering into the world of politics. But a distinguished theologian, of European origin, insisted that we should faithfully inform the churches of the first world, who had given us so much help in that emergency. Otherwise they would think that we had not been honest with them in order to obtain financial help.

An Anglican bishop took up the same position and said, "My church was not involved in the defence of human rights, although it should have been. But we cannot deny to those churches that were committed to that costly struggle the opportunity to share their experiences and beliefs."

Those words tipped the scales in favour of a whole session devoted to human rights, and that evening turned out to be the unforgettable culmination of the meeting for our visitors from all over the world.

Even one of the bishops who had been against such a session finally admitted to me, with tears in his eyes, that he had found it deeply moving and regretted that he had not kept himself duly informed about what had been happening in our country.

It is essential and urgent for us to be aware of what happened in those years of lying, violence and death, if the churches are to be faithful witnesses today in this different critical stage through which we are now passing. Above all, we can no longer remain naïve about "the powers at work behind the masks" (to quote a WCC publication from 1988), nor remain untouched – neither cold nor hot, but lukewarm – by the cry being raised worldwide today for TRUTH, JUSTICE and PEACE. That was the cry of the great prophets, whose message Jesus did not come to destroy but to fulfil in its entirety.

On behalf of our churches, I wish to thank the World Council of Churches, its member churches, the Geneva staff members and, in particular, the author of this book, together with all those who, with him, gave us their support in solidarity during those years, through which we passed in the shadow of the cross, but at the same time, in the unconquerable power of the resurrection.

It is my prayer that this prophetic gospel-inspired testimony will encourage those who come from all over the world to Porto Alegre to respond imaginatively and boldly to the cry which in our days is going out from Brazil, Latin America and the Caribbean to the whole world:

ANOTHER WORLD IS POSSIBLE!

May our response be as passionate as that of the young stewards at our last Central Committee meeting, who recast the theme of our Ninth Assembly in the following words:

GOD, IN YOUR GRACE, HELP US TO TRANSFORM
THE WORLD!

May we – peoples, rulers and churches who claim to be Christian – so act that we can say "We were not disobedient to the heavenly vision."

Emeritus Bishop Federico J. Pagura

Introduction

Vladimir

São Paulo's afternoon traffic was thick and heavy, ground to a halt by its ubiquitous security police. Their orders on that 31 October 1975 were to strangle all access to the city's main Roman Catholic cathedral on the Praça da Sé in the centre of the city. (Ironically, the police dubbed its action Operação Guttenberg.) A precedent-setting ecumenical memorial service, led by Roman Catholic cardinal Paulo Evaristo Arns, alongside officials and representatives of the Jewish, Protestant and Muslim communities, had been publicized to honour the life of Vladimir Herzog, a courageous Jewish journalist who had openly criticized the practices of the entrenched military government in Brazil. Detained by security agents of the Second Army, he had been viciously tortured and had died a few hours later – a "suicide", according to the Army's spokesman.

The traffic clamp-down turned out to be – for the authorities – embarrassingly ineffective. Over eight thousand persons weaved their way through police barricades and kilometres-long traffic jams to the city centre in protest of Herzog's murder and to participate massively in the packed service, spilling out of the filled cathedral onto the *Praça da Sé*.

This singular public event, accompanied by immediate nationwide protests and strikes, marked, according to at least one Brazilian observer, the beginning of the long ten-year process through which, finally, military *de facto* rule gave way to freedom of the press and to a restoration of democratic institutions in the country.[1]

Delia

She was only fifteen years of age. A long tightly woven braid of black hair from her skull had been found and brought by peasants to her grieving mother. The remains of Delia Melgar Quispe and eighteen other Quechua men and women were found in a common grave on a hillside in the municipal district of San Pedro de Chachi in the high Peruvian mountains of Huamanga, Ayacucho. It had just happened. Our ecumenical delegation was confronted immediately with many testimonies from the relatives of these victims, who, with enormous dignity and restraint, told us of the constant threats, disappearances and massacres affecting their indigenous Andean communities, making up the silent majorities of the Peruvian population.

These atrocities, and many others in the early 1990s, had been committed either by members of *Sendero Luminoso* (a violent anti-government insurgency), the Armed Forces and the police, or the civil defense patrols controlled by the Army. We heard and we saw. One man, Zacarias Cconoce Huayhua cried out powerfully in anguish on seeing the body of his wife in the same grave as that of Delia:

"If you had been imprisoned
I could have delivered you.
If you had been ill
I could have healed you.
If you had travelled
I could have visited you.
Now that I see you dead,
I cannot even lay you in a tomb."[2]

Seven Hundred Argentinian children: booty of the "dirty war"

The cover is coloured a gentle beige. The title, "Casos de Niños Detenidos-Desaparecidos y Nacidos en Cautiverio en Argentina desde 1976", deeply disturbing. The contents, chilling. This early 1980 document produced by the Grandmothers *(Abuelas)* of the Plaza de Mayo contains seventy-five pages of sworn testimony and legal depositions in the cold language of the courts: photographs of infants and small children whose parents had been brutally detained by Argentinian security agents or police during the first years of that country's military dictatorship (1976-1983). Even more sinister are those photographs of happy young couples, each couple expecting a child. Most of these estimated 700 "disappeared" boys and girls were taken away from their mothers and fathers and handed by the military in its "dirty war", as booty to childless couples for adoption with false birth certificates. About ten percent of these children have been located and restored, at least morally, to their families. Many of their biological parents, according to recent testimony by an apparently conscience-troubled officer of the Navy, Adolfo Scilingo, were taken after illegal abduction to the infamous Naval Mechanical Centre (ESMA), tortured for days or weeks, then drugged, stripped and dropped alive by military aircraft crews high over the Atlantic Ocean, to their deaths.[3]

Who were these people: the Condor's[4] view of the recent past

Vladimir, Delia and the children in Argentina – these members of the human family – were among the tens of thousands of persons whose lives were violently affected – not as victims of natural disasters – but as victims of the deliberate brutal policies of repression carried out during the decades from the 1960s onwards by Latin American military and authoritarian regimes. It was a terrible and dark period in the history of the Americas.

When did it start?

The end of the Second World War had created great hopes for prosperity in the hemisphere. A new generation cherished radical change, away from old patterns of control and wealth under the traditional ruling elites, in the southern part of the continent as well as in Central America. Earlier, the birth pangs of early industrialization had brought with it sharp demands by workers and peasants for a share in its benefits. There was a shift to urban centres from rural economies and the growth of a powerful work force. Labour unions gradually gained strength. During this period, these new social forces emerged and, inevitably, with economic prosperity in the 1950s just beginning to be felt, laid down fresh political and social challenges. Demands sharpened over the tremendous income disparities between the rich and the poor majorities in both city and rural areas.[5]

These rising post-war unfulfilled expectations, spurred by a new sense of national pride, encouraged attempts to challenge the vested interests of the ruling élites. Programmes of social experiment and reform by social-democrat or socialist governments in such countries as Guatemala, Brazil and Chile elicited much hope among the disenfranchised. The Cuban revolution also represented, for millions of Latin Americans, a viable and effective alternative political model for those without access to basic social economic and cultural rights in the region. Attempts to generate popular political power through guerrilla movements in Brazil, Argentina and Uruguay proved, in the long term, to be counter-productive. Above all, they provided the military castes with a pretext for destroying the basic rights of ordinary citizens, such as freedom of the press, the right to lawful assembly and elections, and, ultimately, freedom from torture and the right to life.

Cold War context

These military takeovers were encouraged and supported, when not actually engineered, by security and military agencies of the United States of America. The Cold War defined the parameters of loyalty and power at that time. Thus, the legitimate aspirations to solve the endemic poverty of the urban and rural poor, expressed through new alliances of the left, political left and centre-left, were perceived to be dangerous threats to the interests of the US and its political allies in the region.

Beginning in the mid-1950s incipient participatory democracies in Latin America were overthrown, one by one, by a military coup. One democratic institution after the other came under the military boot. According to the International Commission of Jurists, these military regimes were "essentially negative, with origins and motivations in the most literal sense, counter-revolutionary... repressing all demo-cratic political activity, liberal and conservative as well as socialist"[6]. Beginning in Paraguay and Guatemala in 1954, followed by Brazil ten years later, elected civilian governments in Uruguay and Chile fell during 1973. Argentina followed in March 1976. Civil liberties, polit-ical pluralism and basic human rights were severely curtailed soon after in Peru, Bolivia and in several Central American countries.

National Security Doctrine

This gave rise to the formulation of a new policy designed to curtail independent movements and parties, barring them from reaching power. This policy was termed the National Security Doctrine (NSD) and became the touchstone of military officers and political advisors of the region. It was further spelled out in May 1981 by the Committee of Santa Fé, designed to set out the strategic policies of the US gov-ernment under the Reagan administration. An important element of US implementation of its actions was that contained in the curricula of the School of the Americas and other army and police training estab-lishments, at which thousands of officers of Latin American armed forces and police agencies received technical and ideological instruc-tion. The armed forces of Brazil became its star pupil, justifying its internal repressive actions from the time it took power in 1964 and especially after 1968. Furthermore, Brazil became the principal agent in exporting and teaching the use of torture in the 1970s, as an instru-ment of interrogation and fear, to its South American neighbours: Par-aguay, Uruguay, Chile, Argentina and Bolivia.

The United States was not the only mentor in Brazil. What is less known is that the French Army's expertise in the use of torture, honed in Vietnam and later during its costly war in Algeria, became a valuable asset for pupils in the Brazilian, Argentinian and Chilean armed forces[7] in the application of repressive measures against their own citizens.

What were its consequences?

The Latin American continent thus experienced a bitter share of state terror. This long chapter of repression – only recently "closed" with the gradual return of formal democratic rule during the 1990s – had witnessed for decades the crushed aspirations of generations of young peasants and students, urban populations and emerging community leaders: generations who thirsted for decent land, education, health and living standards, political participation in decisions affecting them and just governments to ensure their observance.

For their peoples, appalling years followed. Most forms of modern repressive methods of individual and collective rights were standardized. Students, labour unions, professionals and opposition political parties and movements were harassed, persecuted and eliminated. Those who raised their voices, including many in the churches and movements, were silenced. Summary execution in hidden centres of detention became ordinary. Heavy massacres were perpetrated, especially in isolated villages, targeting indigenous communities.

The churches

Church communities in all these countries witnessed and were directly affected by these dramatic events. Many members of the Christian communities and congregations were themselves directly affected by military repression and are to be found among the victims. These included some courageous ordained and lay leaders, both Roman Catholic and Protestant evangelical. The most targeted by official or secret state agencies were those who spoke out against injustice and who identified with the poor.

Member churches of the WCC were among those who stood up against these developments. Not all church leaders or parishes opposed the rigid stability guaranteed under *de facto* military rule, especially among the middle classes.[8] However, a significant number did so. Individuals and congregations, leaders, student and youth groups responded quickly to the suffering and persecution around them.

How did the churches respond to repression?

Their response took many forms. Actions were rapid, efficient and risky, be they to take in people fleeing from neighbouring countries or to hide and protect their own. Many were attacked for standing up to the military. Audacious individuals and congregations, parishes and dioceses in a great number of towns and cities became involved. They issued vibrant calls for a stop to state-perpetrated torture, forced disappearances and death. Increasingly, insistent demands were articulated for a return to the rule of law and the restoration of democratic institutions.

Under military take-overs these "ordinary" people became quickly organized. Small groups of men and women – sometimes, but not always, supported by church leadership – felt compelled to carry out immediate and urgent tasks to protect individuals and families. They devised imaginative ways to assist people to obtain asylum in embassies or to cross dangerous borders. They identified places where missing persons were detained, gathered meticulous information on the nature of violations and publicly denounced reports of torture occurring in these secret locations. They simultaneously attempted to keep hope alive among their own communities and neighbourhoods under harsh restrictive circumstances. Many of that generation were killed for their religious or political convictions. Others died for their testimony and for their defence of the dispossessed. Christians who were involved in this vast popular response against repression gave fresh vitality to a redeemed Church, when she spoke out prophetically and practised justice.

The international ecumenical family was challenged, as rarely before in the Latin American region, to respond to urgent calls for solidarity towards the victims of military repression – early on in Brazil with the first reports of torture, but later massively after the *coup d'état* on 11 September 1973, in Santiago de Chile.

The following story is about the way in which the WCC, a privileged instrument of the worldwide ecumenical family, accompanied those men and women in South America during the *anos de chumbo*.[9]

NOTES

[1] A Vladimir Herzog Human Rights Prize, awarded annually to persons or organizations distinguished for their defence of life and dignity, was inaugurated in 1978 under the auspices of the Roman Catholic Archdiocese of São Paulo. In 1981 the prize was given to

thirty-one Brazilian journalists and organizations of the written press, TV and radio for their "outstanding work this past year in the defence of human rights" (WCC archives).

[2] Quoted in the "Report of an International Ecumenical Delegation to Peru 14-24 October 1990", World Council of Churches, Geneva (WCC archives).

[3] A chilling confession by the former Navy officer in a best-selling book published in 1995: *El Vuelo*, by Horacio Verbitsky (Buenos Aires: Editorial Planeta Argentina)

[4] The deliberate reference to the notorious bird is intended to evoke the symbolism of this unique high-flying Andean vulture. It was also the name of the secret operation planned by Chile's dictator Augusto Pinochet and his southern cone military counterparts to physically eliminate all political opposition in the six countries of this sub-region during the 1970s and 1980s.

[5] See also, for an overview of these realities, the article by Dafne Sabanes Plou, "Latin America", in *A History of the Ecumenical Movement, Vol 3, 1968-2000* (Geneva, WCC Publications, 2004) p566. She writes, "In the early 1960s Latin America was deep in economic, political and social change. The urbanization and industrialization process, which had been growing during the 1950s, increased in the 1960s, bringing with it a rise in urban marginalization... In the political arena, social, labour and student movements grew stronger as the socialist revolution took place in Cuba. A conviction that one could defeat the imperialism imposed by foreign powers and governments in Latin America – particularly by the US – awakened an important social movement."

[6] Cf "Military Regimes in Latin America", in *The Review of the International Commission of Jurists* (Vol.17, December 1976, edited by Niall MacDermot)

[7] "We learned everything from the French", General Albano Harguindeguy, the Argentinian Minister of the Interior under General Videla, is reported to have admitted. The notorious role of French General Aussaresses in Algeria is well documented, including in his autobiography. What is less known is that as military attaché to Brazil he trained Brazilian officers in 1973 in his speciality. Several Chilean officers were similarly taught by him, according to revelations by Manuel Contreras, who was the head of the dreaded secret police in Chile, the DINA. (in *Les Archives du Monde*, 9 avril 2005, p. 77)

[8] Read the analysis of reactionary collaboration, by Ruben Alves, in *Protestantismo e Repressão* (São Paulo: Editora Ática, 1979)

[9] Literally, years of lead, or leaden years, ie under the gun; heavy, depressing, intolerable.

1
What Is This Book About?

Delegates and other members of the worldwide ecumenical family meeting in Brazil for the WCC's Ninth Assembly[1] converge upon a continent where the vast majority, the poor and disadvantaged, are insistently demanding respect for their human dignity and their rightful share of the benefits of the new, rapid growth in many of their nations' economies. This struggle has its roots in the vivid and painful memories of the recent past and in the courageous fight to defend the most basic human right, the right to life itself, under the repressive military dictatorships that ruled most of the nations of the continent during the decades of the 1970s and 1980s.

One can only anticipate the future if we can remember and come to terms with, and apply the lessons of, the past. It is therefore fortunate that the Assembly takes place in Latin America, for nowhere is awareness of the need to preserve the collective memory of the recent past, its crimes and its struggles for justice, more acute.

Memory
This book is therefore above all about that memory.

It seeks to help members of the present generation to understand the continuing struggle of the churches and people of this continent as they ferret out, come to grips with and make known the truth about decades of infamy. Succeeding generations must never again be subjected to such systematic and abject criminal acts at the hands of the State or any other power. This is a story of remarkable faith and courage: where the victims found the courage to tell the truth about systematic brutal torture, personal humiliation and the murder or disappearance of their loved ones; and where the churches and other groups stood with them courageously during the darkest years of the recent past and told their truth at home and abroad. It is a story of hope generated by ordinary men and women who constantly rise up in unexpected ways in each generation to continue to work, extraordinarily, for righteousness.

It also aims at strengthening the ecumenical memory of this region's struggle for human rights – especially for the benefit of a younger generation that is largely unaware of this chapter of ecumenical history. It describes how the churches and others around the world, through the World Council of Churches, accompanied *(acom-panharam[2])* South American churches and human rights groups during these two harsh decades of military rule in the continent, and subsequently in their continuing struggle against impunity for past crimes.

The churches...

In the 1960s and early 1970s military regimes replaced elected civilian governments throughout Latin America. In the following years, individual members of the Christian communities – a proportionately small sector of those in society opposed to military rule – were harassed, detained, persecuted and driven into exile. Hundreds of thousands of ordinary persons were massacred in Central America, and many thousands of persons became victims of forced disappearance and murder at the hands of the military, as occurred in Argentina. In face of this systematic campaign of official terror, the Latin American churches called for effective, urgent manifestations of international ecumenical solidarity – pastoral, political, material and financial – to enable them to protect and assist those persons and communities targeted individually and collectively by the military regimes in their countries.

... with the international ecumenical family

This brief volume describes how the member churches and staff of the WCC worked together in seven countries of South America to meet that challenge. A long-standing basic working principle of the WCC was applied, namely that its actions should be taken in response to and after consultation with its member churches. This guideline proved to be of critical importance during the period when the physical integrity and lives of so many were at stake. The WCC followed the lead of its strong membership principally in the seven countries considered here: Brazil, Uruguay, Chile, Argentina, Paraguay, Bolivia and Peru. Thus the following narrative concentrates on the struggle for human rights and the defence of life where the constituency of the WCC was most strongly present and active.

The WCC also responded to urgent needs in some other countries in the region such as Colombia, Ecuador or Venezuela, where WCC membership was weak or non-existent. Other ecumenical partners – local, regional or international – acted efficiently to meet these urgent needs in these cases. They also provided critical information and guidance for WCC supportive action to be mobilized when it was needed. Broad ecumenical response was not always possible, however. Several dioceses of the Roman Catholic Church in different parts of Latin America – especially in Chile or Brazil – provided indispensable institutional backing for innovative ecumenical initiatives alongside Protestant evangelical churches and individual leaders to defend and promote human rights. The *Vicaría de la Solidaridad* of the Archdiocese of Santiago, Chile, was a particularly notable case in point.

During the 1980s, designated representatives from the churches and ecumenical human rights groups from Central America and the Caribbean region, including the Caribbean Conference of Churches (CCC) and the region-wide ecumenical human rights network, Caribbean Rights, participated fully in the regional consultations convened by the WCC in collaboration with the newly-formed Latin American Council of Churches (CLAI).

However, the rich experience of solidarity of the WCC alongside the Central American and Caribbean churches and ecumenical organizations is only briefly referred to in this book, given the distinct history of Indigenous and AfroCaribbean peoples and the specific social and geopolitical constraints and challenges facing the populations and the churches in that region. The record of the struggle for human rights in Mesoamerica and the Caribbean region merits the full attention of the ecumenical community. It is to be hoped that the distinguished record of the ecumenical cooperation in the struggle for human rights will soon be fully narrated.

Additional resources

This book intends, therefore, to suggest ways by which new ecumenical generations might look into the recent past. For those who would like to pursue work in this area the archives of the WCC library in Geneva provide rich material. Most of the material upon which this book is based is to be found there. The Declaration of the Eighth Assembly of the WCC on the occasion of the 50th anniversary of the signing of the Universal Declaration of Human Rights, is in Appendix I. A list of human rights organizations with whom the WCC collaborated most closely is in Appendix II. Appendix III contains a bibliography with additional resources on the history of Latin America during this period. Since the most credible and reliable data on the past and present human rights situations and challenges in each country are to be found in documentation centres and institutions set up by those who have been directly involved in the human rights struggle, an up-to-date list of additional archival sources in Latin America is provided in Appendix IV.

NOTES

[1] In Porto Alegre, in the state of Rio Grande do Sul, 14-23 February 2006.
[2] This evocative word, used daily in Brazilian Portuguese, signifies "being together with" (as alongside a travel companion or a person of trust), "follow" (go in the same direction), "associate with" (to harbour the same conviction), "escort" (as to an event), or "provide harmony for" (as when playing a guitar). In this context, the word conveys deep pastoral overtones of solidarity.

2
Never Again
Brazil

The revelation of the death by torture of journalist Vladimir Herzog in 1975 took Brazil by storm. The huge public outcry that followed confronted society and especially the public media with a reality, hitherto taboo: agencies of the military government that ruled the country from 1964-1985 were torturing its citizens and causing its suspected opponents to disappear.

The *coup d'état* on 1 April 1964 installed a regime that radically curtailed the basic human rights of citizens. Democratic institutions were severely weakened or abolished. During the succeeding two decades well over 20,000 citizens were imprisoned, often without charges, and many of them brutally tortured. Some were killed outright or died in captivity. Some 150 persons were forcibly "disappeared" – a relatively low number by later Latin American standards. Many thousands of persons were driven into exile.

Guido Rocha was one of the victims. A gifted artist, he was imprisoned several times during the 1960s for his depiction of military abuses in paintings and political cartoons. After fleeing to Chile as a refugee he created a series of dramatic sculptured figures of the crucified Christ, based on his own experiences of torture by the police. Following the 1973 military coup in Santiago, he once again fled and was granted refugee status in Switzerland, where he received a grant to work at the School of Fine Arts in Geneva. It was there that he prepared his largest work – a stark figure of a twisted, gaunt contemporary man in the throes of torture – and donated it to the WCC as a gesture of appreciation for the churches' part in helping him and other refugees to flee for their lives from Chile.

Rocha's work illustrates his "own obsession with the Crucifixion as the symbol of Christ's suffering, where his figures confront you brutally and directly with agony"[1]. The gripping work confronted visitors to the Ecumenical Centre in Geneva for a year before it was shipped for exhibit at the WCC's Fifth Assembly in Nairobi, Kenya, in 1975. There it became a symbol of the horrors being discovered by Christians and churches in Latin America and other parts of the world, and of the faith that was giving them the courage to engage in costly solidarity.

In Brazil itself, the Roman Catholic Church was particularly articulate in denouncing these injustices. The roles of leaders like Dom Helder Camara, Archbishop of Recife, and of Dom Paulo Evaristo Arns, Cardinal Archbishop of São Paulo, were soon recognized universally. They were not alone, however. A significant number of other Brazilian Catholic bishops and Protestant leaders and laypersons also spoke out bravely against repression or worked quietly all across the country to comfort victims, to aid prisoners and their families, to intervene with the authorities, to strengthen new democratic movements of resistance and to call for a return to the rule of law.

In addition to denouncing the systematic use of torture by the government, increasing concern was expressed about the widespread violation of the economic and other human rights of marginalized groups targeted for severe repression by the police and paramilitary forces: indigenous groups *(nações Índias)*, workers, landless peasants, black communities and women living in abject poverty.

The WCC had already developed close relationships with its member churches in Brazil in the 1950s, particularly in the area of youth and student work, Christian education and health programmes. It was thus alerted early after the 1964 military takeover to the repression of dissent within their midst by some Protestant communities, particularly by the leadership of the Presbyterian Church of Brazil (IPB). Its authoritarian policies at the time led to the imprisonment or exile of a number of able pastors and lay leaders[2] after 1968 when Institutional Act Number 5 was decreed. Giving expression to the worldwide ecumenical concern about these developments, the international ecumenical family, and the WCC in particular, reached out to cooperate with those Roman Catholic archdioceses and dioceses sensitive to the needs of those most affected by military rule.

The WCC also strengthened its links with the new ecumenical leadership emerging in Brazil, closely related to the progressive churches. It gave particular support to the Church and Society Movement (*Iglesia y Sociedad en América Latina* – ISAL)[3] whose representatives had made dramatic contributions to the WCC's World Conference on Church and Society held in Geneva in 1966. In cooperation with other secular and church movements in the early 1970s, they circulated some of the first reports of illegal detention and torture being perpetrated in the country.[4] These solidly documented reports were shared rapidly with churches and other international organizations outside Brazil.

A ten-page substantiated document dated 22 July 1970 had been submitted by a clandestine network of Brazilian lawyers, historians and dissident diplomats to the Geneva-based International Commission of Jurists and the WCC. Entitled *Relatório sobre a repressão policial e torturas infligidas à oposição e prisioneiros politicos no Brasil*, it provided an important source, among others, for a submission to the Commission on Human Rights of the United Nations, in Geneva, on 23 March 1971, alerting it to a "consistent pattern of violations of Human Rights, including torture" in Brazil, by WCC's Commission of the Churches on International Affairs, along with the World Federation of Trade Unions, the International Commission of Jurists and Pax Romana.[5] Simultaneously, members of the ecumenical community in Brazil began discreetly to accompany and assist political prisoners and their families located in the industrialized south of Brazil as well as in the Northeast, a process which rapidly set a pattern of often secret, efficient cooperation with the WCC from early on under the military dictatorship.

During the mid-1970s the WCC energetically engaged in solidarity with the churches and people of Brazil, pursuing a two-pronged approach: sharing information on abuses and torture with churches around the world, with appropriate United Nations bodies, and with concerned governments abroad; and the provision of direct moral and financial assistance to detainees and prisoners through ecumenical channels inside Brazil. It recognized that this largest of Roman Catholic constituencies in the world, in light of the severe curtailment of freedom of expression, was becoming the main national "voice of the voiceless", and that it was uniquely placed to provide the space and protection not only for the victims but also for the non-violent opponents of the military regime and thus merited the full attention and support of the international ecumenical family.

Brazil is a vast country (covering half of the South American continent), with a population of over 182 million persons. On 1 April 1964 the Armed Forces of the country took over power from the elected government of João Goulart. It then ruled until 1985 when, under strong popular demands for a return to democracy, it ceded power to a civilian administration. With the application of Institutional Act No. 5, issued on 15 December 1968 the country experienced a regime of terror under a system which allowed the head of government to suspend Congress and ban the right of Habeas Corpus for any citizen. As a result elected officials were dismissed and any person's political rights could be abrogated for up to ten years. When armed guerrilla groups were organized on ill-fated campaigns to oust the military, by 1973 they were soon crushed and served as a pretext for the armed forces to clamp down further on thousands of student activists, labour leaders, members of political parties and church leaders who spoke up against the regime's practices. Press and radio media were tightly censored. In the name of national security, up to twenty-thousand persons were detained, most of whom were systematically tortured, of which one hundred and fifty persons are known to have been forcibly disappeared. While the early years of military rule brought economic and industrial growth to the country, with increased international investment and exports, it did not benefit the tens of millions of poor people of Brazil. After the return to civilian rule in 1985, torture had become what many observers qualify as endemic and routine, practised systematically, especially in police stations. Off-duty police made up death squads which still operated into the 1990s seeking out street children. The killings of rioting common law prisoners was a regular occurrence. With the election of Fernando Henrique Cardoso in 1994, inflation was brought under effective control. In addition, an innovative programme of land distribution for poor peasants was initiated under his administration. The Amazon basin became a sharpened focus of increased attention, as indigenous Indian leaders protested at the eroding rights of their tribes, faced with racism, expulsion and disease. Since 2004 a government of the political left has been headed by Luiz Inácio da Silva (Lula, as he is widely known), creating high expectations among the poor majority electorate. Despite recent accusations of corruption in the PT (Workers' Party) and the slow pace with which promised land reform is being implemented, Lula's personal popularity continues strong.

CLAMOR

In the early and mid-1970s, refugees from Argentina, Uruguay and Chile made their way onto Brazilian soil across permeable borders, especially after the *coup d'état* in Chile on 11 September 1973. A special team, CLAMOR[6], was set up by the Archdiocese of São Paulo to receive persons who did not wish to make their presence known to the authorities. Confronted with the alarming accounts of the increasing incidence of forced disappearance of persons from their homes, workplaces, or schools, and of the existence of often clandestine detention centers in countries of the "southern cone", CLAMOR began to publish reliable reports of human rights abuses throughout this region in close cooperation with emerging new human rights organizations there.[7] The early commitment of this remarkable team[8] in putting into practice their slogan, "solidarity has no frontiers"[9], had a distinct influence on the evolving tactics adopted by the WCC in responding to urgent human rights needs in the region: use discretion, be accurate, act rapidly and always in symbiosis with ecumenical partners and the churches.

CESE (Ecumenical Coordination Service)

Simultaneously, a vast campaign was launched across Brazil through CESE[10] – the national ecumenical service agency founded in 1973 – to make the Universal Declaration of Human Rights (UDHR) widely known to members of the churches and to the wider citizenship. The thirty articles of the Declaration were published by CESE in 1975, accompanied by biblical quotations and theological references from both the Protestant and Roman Catholic traditions. A little under two million copies were printed and circulated among the churches in every single state of this vast country. It proved to be a powerful pedagogical instrument for helping ordinary Christians to become aware of their individual and collective rights and responsibilities, and to equip them spiritually and morally for decisive action to promote human dignity in cooperation with other non-governmental organizations and growing civil society movements throughout Brazil. CESE's initiative, taken with the full support of the WCC, was rapidly picked up by church bodies in Latin America, North America and Europe who produced similar publications, adapted for their own constituencies.[11]

Landless peasants in the North

Article 17 of the UDHR, with its biblical reference (Genesis 34:10) to the right of each person to enjoy access to land, attracted the attention of more than one poor farmer who happened to lay his hands on CESE's publication. Pastors and laypeople of the Evangelical Church of Lutheran Confession in Brazil, one of the strong member churches of the WCC, have struggled with their own history and developed their own understanding of the ownership and use of the land, one of the central issues of Brazil, past and present. The gradual conversion of its leadership from a neutral position in the 1970s with respect to military rule[12] to that of an outspoken defender of the land rights of peasants and indigenous peoples is worthy of note. It occurred in the context of an animated internal debate in the church between Lutheran big land-owners on the one hand and Lutheran small farmers and peasant families on the other, which raised awareness within the whole church itself and led it to come to terms with its constituencies' needs.[13] Actions by some of its pastors among poor farmers in the South as well as in the vast regions of Northeast Brazil on land traditionally inhabited by indigenous "nations" subsequently focused the attention of this member church increasingly on the need for structural, economic and political reform in Brazil.

This experience also served to give impetus to the creation of channels by which landless peasants could defend themselves against the violent attacks by gunmen hired by large landowners, and the corrupt judicial systems imbedded especially in several states of the North and Northwest. It also encouraged the WCC to be attentive to the early, and already controversial, initiatives taken by organized landless peasant communities, notably through the *Movimento dos Trabalhadores Rurais Sem Terra* (MST), to invade fallow land. The Council responded rapidly to some of this movement's first appeals for international financial help and enabled its leadership to gain access to the sessions of the United Nations Commission on Human Rights.

Workers in the South

The overarching effect of the military's economic policies during its first decade and a half in power was that the "miracle" which it espoused was more friendly to foreign investment and to a growing urban middle class than to Brazil's majority population. Its viability depended not only on a vast relocation of peasants to the Amazon so as to make room for agro-industries, but also on a muzzled labour force in the growing urban industrial sector. Since workers' wages decreased under inflation and they could not count on minimal social rights, by the end of the 1970s they had begun openly to challenge the military's policies, with profound social and political ramifications.

On 30 March 1980, over 60,000 members of the labour movement in the State of São Paulo, led by Luis Inácio da Silva *(Lula)* decided to stop work following the refusal of the auto industries to accept their demands for job security, union representation in management, union autonomy and the right to strike. Two weeks later, on 18 April, helmeted squadrons of the military police violently attacked these striking metal workers in São Paulo's industrial park of São Bernardo do Campo. National and international reaction was swift, denouncing the use of force against workers with *bona fide* demands .

Five days after the strike had begun, a significant number of Protestant pastors, mobilized by two leaders of the Methodist Church of Brazil, Bishop Paulo Ayres Mattos and Nelson Luiz Campos Leite[14], were among those who rapidly took a public stand in solidarity with the workers:

> We, who are inspired by the teachings of the Gospel of our Lord Jesus, ... affirm the right of all sectors of society to full and free participation in national decision-making, and reject all acts of arbitrary character and repression. We express our solidarity with the striking metal workers and with those at their side as they seek better living conditions, work and effective participation at all levels of national life. The struggle of the *metalúrgicos* is part of a larger struggle in which other sectors of Brazilian society are involved in constructing a more just society. (...). We feel a close fraternity with the positions taken by the Catholic Church through the witness of its bishops, priests and lay people who have publicly stood alongside the workers in their struggle for legitimate rights.

The entire Catholic Conference of Brazilian Bishops also took a clear stand protesting against the military's repressive acts against the workers and in favour of their legitimate claims. The Catholic bishop of the Santo André and São Bernardo diocese where the industrial park was located, Monsignor Claudio Hummes, underlined especially the urgent need to provide spiritual and material assistance to the workers and their families so that they might take their decisions in full freedom without constraints of hunger or police harassment.

With this confrontation coming as it did at a time when the generals wished to portray themselves as being open to more democracy, the union appealed to the international community to acknowledge the movement's moral legitimacy and to assist workers' families during the strike. Beyond this, they sought support for their efforts to create alternative political parties more reflective of popular needs. (The infant Workers' Party, the PT, was then in full cry.) In response to this appeal, WCC General Secretary Philip Potter made provisions for material assistance to be made available to the families of striking workers. In his accompanying letter (23 June 1980) to Cardinal Paulo Evaristo Arns, Potter emphasized that he and his colleagues felt "encouraged and stimulated by your firm Christian witness, as well as that of the National Conference of Brazilian Bishops, in supporting the legitimate demands of the metal workers in the Archdiocese of São Paulo." He went on to write that

> your decisive support to those sectors of society which have not benefitted from the so-called *abertura democrática* challenges the world Christian community to elicit words and gestures of solidarity with you. On recommendation of representatives of the member churches of the WCC in Brazil, emergency grants were made to meet the subsistence needs of the families of the workers on strike at the ABC.

He later received a delegation of the movement, with *Lula* at its head, at the WCC's headquarters in Geneva.

Brasil Nunca Mais

Without a doubt no public action marked Brazilian national awareness of and commitment to human rights more deeply than the audacious project called *Brasil: Nunca Mais* (BNM) *(Brazil: Never Again)*. Under the courageous leadership, protection and sponsorship of Cardinal Paulo Evaristo Arns, a small group of committed lawyers, researchers and writers obtained clandestinely the official records of military courts over a six-year period and used them to expose the full panoply of torture and repressive instruments which the successive military regimes had employed against those it suspected of being political opponents. From 1979 to 1985, under the strictest secrecy, the WCC obtained and channeled the full financial resources required for the success of this project.

This extraordinary story started with a mid-1978 visit to WCC Geneva headquarters by Eny Raimundo Moreira, a Brazilian lawyer based in Rio de Janeiro. Her defence of political prisoners under the severe restrictions imposed by the military on the civilian courts at the time had endeared her to them, to their families and their friends. Recommended to us by André Jacques, then director of refugee services of CIMADE, in France[15], whom she had visited earlier, Eny was deeply concerned that court records in Brazil, and in particular the testimony of the accused, might be destroyed, never be made public as part of the Brazilian historical record, or be simply forgotten. The project which she brought to the WCC, on behalf of a group of lawyers of similar experience and vision, called for a team to collect systematically the available records of past and current trials of political detainees and prisoners being held in civil or military courts, so as to form the basis of a historical record to be published when circumstances allowed.[16]

It was a risky venture and, to be successful, it required considerable financial support. Would the WCC help? During the following days the idea was discussed by a small group of colleagues, including the General Secretary. The project was approved on one condition: that it be protected by a sufficiently wide Brazilian "umbrella" of impeccable credibility and institutional strength so as to ensure its viability and the physical integrity of those carrying it out. The Archdiocese of São Paulo became that umbrella. The project had already been brought to the attention of Cardinal Arns, who immediately recognized the historical import of the scheme as well as members of the CLAMOR team. Immediately the Rev. Jaime Wright was requested by Dom Paulo to assume the overall coordination of its implementation. By early 1979 it was off the ground.

Five trusted persons were carefully chosen for their professional competence, seriousness and confidentiality to carry out the project. Of the five, four are now publicly identified: Paulo Vanucchi, who directed the whole operation; Luis-Eduardo Greenhalgh, Luis Carlos Sigmarina Seixas and, of course, Eny Moreira. They were invited to organize, at first, the initial phase of obtaining and photocopying the first official records of the hundreds of military court trials which had been held since 1964. By the end of 1979 the project was in full swing – under the greatest of secrecy.

Driven by their shared commitment that the kidnappings, torture, forced disappearances, murders, and institutionalized terror must never again be allowed to occur in Brazilian society, this team spent the next six years of their lives working assiduously and with great courage. They had three objectives in mind: to preserve the memory of what happened during the dictatorship, based entirely on official documentation of military justice; to denounce the causes of repression; and to work to multiply instruments to achieve justice.

Under their strict guidance an expanded team of thirty-five researchers worked in small teams to scrutinize thousands of documents from more than 707 trials that had taken place over a fifteen-year period, most of them military. To gain access to these records, lawyers recruited by the managing team, and working voluntarily, photocopied more than a million pages of court records. Each evening at closing time they would quite legally and systematically sign out the records of each trial at a court archival office, then spend all night in an unpretentious office elsewhere, quite illegally photocopying them before returning them to the files the next morning.

This went on for a year, astonishingly with no suspicions raised. Based on these documents, the team carried on for the next four years to produce a 6891-page, twelve-volume series documenting over 200 types of torture, 242 secret torture centres and identifying 444 individual torturers by name and pseudonym – all gleaned and cross-checked from official records. The volumes include distinct studies of the descriptions of methods of torture applied at that time. They name the specific armed services, police forces and security agencies responsible for torture. They describe the repressive laws used to justify torture. They list the victims and the categorization of the social groups targeted. Finally they describe and identify, from the material extrapolated from the court testimony and documents, the history and rationale of those movements and organizations of the political left that had opposed and fought against the military regime[17].

As the work progressed, the team was keenly aware of the danger of discovery by the military police at any time. They worked in a number of nondescript buildings provided to them by the Catholic church, with row upon row of boxes containing the original photocopies, as well as a battery of computers used by individual researchers to analyze them. To back up their work all the files were regularly and systematically microfilmed and secretly smuggled out of the country to Geneva[18].

It was in 1985 that the final stage of the project was reached: that of publishing its condensed findings in a book, drafted in popular language, but anonymously, by two well-known Brazilian authors: Ricardo Kotscho and Frei Beto. The result, a 312-page book entitled *Brasil Nunca Mais*, appeared in bookstores all across the country in July of that year. It describes in bold and chilling detail the individual stories of horror as had been told by each victim in court and meticulously recorded by a stenographer, as well as the history and the structure of military oppression in Brazil. Prefaced by both Cardinal Paulo Evaristo Arns and WCC General Secretary Philip Potter[19], it became an immediate best-seller.

This seminal work produced a socio-political explosion in Brazilian society. At the time (1985) it was the most complete and accurate account of torture in Brazil and still remains the reference-point. Its publisher, *Editora Vozes*, had to run off thirty-four printings of the book, at ten thousand copies each, to meet public demand. It sold more copies than any other nonfiction book in the history of Brazilian publishing and remained on the list of bestsellers for ninety-one consecutive weeks. Its significance and impact can be measured by the astounding number of articles and reviews – over one thousand - elicited by it over the past twenty years, mostly in Brazil, but also in other regions of the world[20]. Its translation into English[21] stimulated a major literary magazine in the USA, *The New Yorker*[22], to dedicate two issues exclusively to the *process* by which the research had been carried out. Its insights were then fully developed in a book[23] by the same author (in which he describes as well the story behind the writing of Uruguay's *Nunca Mas*)[24]. In turn, the book was translated into Portuguese. Such was the interest generated by the work of this unusual Brazilian team.

Most importantly, however, the research and publication resulting from the BNM gambit contributed greatly to making the public aware of the practice of torture, especially among the young generation which grew up under military rule – precisely because it was a literal account of what occurred in Brazil, rather than an exhortation[25]. Only two months after the first edition of *Brasil Nunca Mais* was published, the government led by José Sarney, the first elected civilian president after the military regime gave up power in 1985, resolved to sign, on 23 September at the United Nations headquarters in New York, the UN Convention against Torture and Other Cruel, Inhuman or Degrading Treatment or Punishment. Whether it was taken by coincidence or under public pressure, this significant decision was nonetheless lauded by the community of human rights advocates in the country.

The book also introduced new ethical and historical criteria by which political and military leaders of the country were subsequently brought to account for their past actions, or at least socially and morally stigmatized for what they had done. Civil servants in various states of the country were forced to resign when it became known that they were former torturers, persons whose names were identified in what was popularly known as "the Cardinal's list". In some cases, as in Ceará, Pará and the Federal District in Brasilia, the men who had earlier been involved in torture were rejected by the Minister of Justice under Fernando Henrique Cardoso as candidates for overseeing Federal Police units[26]. Many were denounced, shunned, or expelled from their professional associations[27].

Two concluding comments

Beyond the lessons alluded to above, for example, the importance of building solidarity across political frontiers and geographic borders, the WCC's experience in accompanying these cutting-edge initiatives in Brazil helped us to gain at least two valuable insights into how to act together with the churches and human rights groups in other regions of the hemisphere.

In the first place, Brazil taught us that it is a gift of the Spirit, in a continent with a majority of Roman Catholics, that Christians have worked together ecumenically when it comes to defending the dignity of persons and defending life itself. Despite the past, troubled history of relations between Catholic and Protestant Evangelicals – as difficult, harmful and sensitive these relations have been during the past centuries in the region[28] – the prophetic and pastoral actions of a certain proportion of Catholic leadership, religious orders and laypeople in the defence of human rights, as illustrated in Brazil, have challenged the member churches of the WCC and the international ecumenical family in the past three decades. One can affirm, in fact, that the record of the two progressive minorities of both Christian traditions working together (some Catholic dioceses and some Protestant communities) has not only contributed to strengthening the human rights movement but considerably enriched social thought. The threat today is that the experiences of the joint ecumenical struggle for justice will be forgotten and weakened by the neo-fundamentalists in both camps.

In the second place, the success and impact of the BNM project encouraged the WCC to follow and support other similar initiatives by church-related human rights groups in the Latin American region. During the delicate transition periods from military rule to civilian government, (self) amnesty laws were passed in various countries as a condition of a return to democracy. These laws, in effect, protected thousands of military violators of human rights from being tried by law for their offences, many of which were considered crimes against humanity, as was the case in Brazil. It became imperative, therefore, that the testimonies of victims and of their families be recorded in some fashion and that the truth of what had occurred during the repressive period of military rule in some other countries be published and become officially recognized. Thus, *Nunca Más!* (Never Again!) publications sprouted up in several countries during the 1980s. Some were officially sponsored and carried out, as in Argentina, Chile, Guatemala and El Salvador. The WCC paid close attention to the *Nunca Más* efforts initiated by non-governmental organizations and the churches, and actively supported some of the teams that carried them out[29].

NOTES

[1] *One World* (WCC's monthly magazine), December 1974, p. 19.

[2] See the monograph by João Dias de Araújo, *Inquisição sem Fogueiras: Vinte anos de História da Igreja Presbiteriana do Brasil: 1954-1974* (São Paulo: Instituto Superior de Estudos da Religião-ISER, 1976).

[3] As we shall see below in other chapters, this region-wide Church-related ecumenical movement provided lucid and courageous leadership to churches and groups in a number of other countries in Latin America as they were confronted with violent military rule in the seventies, affecting a wide spectrum of society. Leaders and members of ISAL, as well as its sister ecumenical organizations MEC (Student Christian Movement), ULAJE (the Latin American Union of Evangelical Youth), and CELADEC (the Latin American Protestant Commission for Christian Education), with the increasing cooperation of UNELAM (Evangelical Committee on Christian Unity in Latin America) contributed keen orientation and strength to the early initiatives of the churches to protect refugees and defend the human rights of ordinary citizens in most of the countries surveyed in this review. Under persecution during the worst of repression in the 1970s, these pioneering ecumenical organizations were re-organized under a new umbrella, the Latin American ecumenical social action (ASEL), with headquarters in Mexico.

[4] This voluminous information, carefully disguised, was flown personally to New York to four concerned members of the Brazilian ecumenical community (Rubem César Fernandez, Domicio dos Mattos, Jether Pereira Ramalho, and Jovelino Ramos) and was brought to the attention of the Rev. William Wipfler, Director of the Latin America Desk of the National Council of Churches of Christ in the USA. Immediately a first published report, entitled *Terror in Brazil: a Dossier*, based on this information, was compiled with the cooperation of Mr. Thomas Quigley, Assistant Director of the Division for Latin America of the US Catholic Conference, and the Brazilian academics Brady Tyson and Ralph della Cava. This dossier was widely distributed to alert the churches, the press, the academic community and members of the US Congress to these startling developments in Brazil.

[5] Accessible in WCC archives.

[6] Not an acronym. Its designation alludes to the Psalmist's clamor for help from the Lord: "Let my prayer come before thee, incline thy ear to my cry!" (Ps. 88:1-2).

[7] See the full story of this intrepid team under the auspices of the Archdiocese of São Paulo, entitled *CLAMOR: A Vitória de Uma Conspiração Brasileira*, written by Samarone Lima (Editora Objetiva Ltda., 2003). Cf especially the preface written by Cardinal Paulo Evaristo Arns.

[8] Jan Rocha, Luiz Eduardo Greenhalgh and the Rev. Jaime Wright

[9] The full quote, attributed to Jaime Wright, goes as follows: "We have learned that the concern for the human being cannot be limited by geographical, political, linguistic, religious or ideological borders. In other words, we have learned that solidarity has no frontiers".

[10] CESE: Ecumenical Coordinating Service Group.

[11] Within a short period the specific articles of the UDHR, accompanied by biblical references, theological reflections or statements by Catholic or Protestant church bodies, were reproduced and adapted by churches, parishes and ecumenical organizations in Chile (published by the Vicaria de la Solidaridad), in Argentina (by the Movimiento Ecuménico por los Derechos Humanos), in Paraguay (by the monthly *Acción*), and eventually for the entire region by the Latin American Council of Churches (CLAI) for its Protestant Evan-

gelical membership. Versions also appeared in Canada (English) and in Switzerland (French). An interesting translation of the UDHR was published in popular Guaraní, *(Ñane Ñe'êt)*, but without commentaries, by the Paraguayan organizations CEDHU (Centro de Estudios Humanitarios) and BASE-ISEC. (Original copies of these and other versions of the commented UDHR are accessible in WCC archives).

[12] General Ernesto Geisel, one of the earlier leaders (1974-1978) of the military regime was a prominent member of the IECLB, (Evangelical Church of Lutheran Confession in Brazil).

[13] Cf the testimony of the Rev. Inacio Lemke, the (then) vice-president of the Pastoral Commission of the Land (CPT), in an article written by Conny Sjöberg entitled "Land Struggle in Brazil leads to New Theological Concepts" (*Lutheran World Information* 8/88): "The struggle for the right to land for small farmers and landless peasants in Brazil is beginning to have a real impact on the theology of our churches".

[14] Along with 44 other pastors and lay members of the Methodist, Presbyterian, Reformed, Congregational, Lutheran and Episcopal churches.

[15] The French ecumenical service agency founded, in 1939, by the lay theologian Suzanne de Diétrich.

[16] Eny Raimundo Moreira, can therefore, justifiably and historically, be remembered as the original "mother of the idea" behind *Brasil Nunca Mais*, which was successfully adopted, adapted and implemented by Cardinal Paulo Evaristo Arns and his team. This fact has not sufficiently been taken into account by the custodians and interpreters of its official history, if at all. Significantly, the central figure of the five-person team – the man who actually directed it - Paulo Vanucchi, attributes more importance to Ms Moreira's role than his own and said so publicly: see the interview by Zuenir Ventura in *Jornal do Brasil*, 25 August 1990, Secção Idéias/Livros, p.6.

[17] The WCC library is the only institution located in Europe which possesses the full set of twelve volumes containing the "universe" of data and analyses of the records of the military courts.

[18] Donated to, and ultimately safeguarded, at the request of the São Paulo Archdiocese, at the Center for Research Libraries in Chicago, Illinois, USA..

[19] The full story of this adventure is well written by Joan Dassin, in a preface to the English version of *Brasil Nunca Mais*, published in the USA as *Torture in Brazil: A Report by the Archdiocese of São Paulo* (New York: Random House, 1986 -first edition; Austin: University of Texas, 1998 – second edition].

[20] Photocopies of all the articles and reviews from 1985 to 2000 are accessible in the WCC archives

[21] *Torture in Brazil* (New York: Vintage Books/Random House, 1986).

[22] *The New Yorker* magazine, issues of May 25 and June 1, 1987, in an article written by Lawrence Weschler.

[23] Weschler, Lawrence, *A Miracle, A Universe*. See Appendix III: Bibliography.

[24] Published by the Servicio Paz y Justica in Uruguay. See Bibliography.

[25] WCC's member churches had been made aware, to a certain extent, of the "Statement on Torture" adopted and disseminated by its Central Committee in 1977. As part of the recommendations it makes, it urges the churches to "intensify their efforts to inform their members and the people of their nations about the provisions of the Universal Declaration of Human Rights, and especially of its Article 5, which reads: 'No one shall be subjected to torture or to cruel, inhuman or degrading treatment or punishment' " (*The Churches in International Affairs/CCIA-WCC/Reports 1974-1978*, p. 30).

[26] Wright, op cit.

[27] Such as Amilcar Lobo, a physician who had closely monitored victims' capacity to endure torture sessions in military barracks without dying.

[28] The author has himself painful childhood recollections of a time (late 1930s) when a priest-led mob threw stones at a Protestant evangelical student choir directed by his mother in the main square of a town located in the state of Minas Gerais.

[29] e.g. *Chile Memoria Prohibida* (Chile); *El Precio de la Paz* (Paraguay); *Juicio de Garcia Meza* (Bolivia). See bibliography Appendix III.

3

The Island
Uruguay

For more than half a century Uruguayans had enjoyed, since the early 1900s, a long and prosperous exercise of a vigorous liberal democratic system, guaranteeing for all its citizens the enjoyment of civil and political rights (including voting rights for women), evident social harmony and the benefits of a generous welfare state. However, in the 1950s and into the next decade standards of living fell due to the stagnation of economic growth. Inflation helped to create a climate of unrest and strikes became frequent. Government repression, which until 1966 was incipient and sporadic, became directly apparent. The press was curtailed and protests repressed. The suspension of civil liberties and the imposition of economic policies disastrous for the population generated even greater popular resistance. In the late 1960s an urban guerrilla group, the Tupamaros[1], carried out spectacular violent actions designed to overthrow the elected government and to replace it with one which would resolve the economic crisis then shaking the country. These tactics of violence provided the armed forces of Uruguay with the pretext to take power and to subvert the historic institutions which were guaranteed by the constitution. The authoritarian regime of the state of emergency became permanent under President Juan Bordaberry, elected in 1972. He was forced to resign by the military establishment in July 1973.

Deprivation and cruelty

The description of what followed over the next twelve years in Uruguay is sobering and eloquent. Thousands were arrested, tortured, and imprisoned for years. Forced disappearances and deaths occurred regularly. More political prisoners were incarcerated there, in proportion to the population of three million persons, than in any other country in Latin America.

The *Servicio Paz y Justicia – Uruguay* (SERPAJ), one of the most effective human rights organizations in the country, describes this situation best, in the preface to its notable 360-page report covering that period[2]:

> The "war" in Uruguay produced nothing so spectacular as the bombing of Government House by Pinochet in Chile or the genocide committed by the military juntas in Argentina when thousands disappeared. But in Uruguay it was carried out with unprecedented sophistication; it was a hushed, progressive repression measured out in doses until it gained absolute control over the entire population. Our country was occupied by our own army, and we Uruguayans were made impotent and defenceless before an uncontrolled despotic will. Even humanitarian acts and expressions of solidarity became targets for accusations of subversion. Helping a torture victim or finding relief for a relative of a political prisoner or a relative of someone who had disappeared could be called "assistance by association to commit a crime". This was our "war"; a war in which the armed forces admit to having lost their "points of reference"; an undocumented war, without clear enemies; a war in which acts of service, the defense of national security, and patriotism were confused with immorality, a breakdown in ethics, and crime. The "dirty war" turned into common criminality, guaranteeing a national security system that no one had elected. And the business worked well: the actors performed with impunity.

According to the records examined by SERPAJ when it produced its survey, from testimony it received from former prisoners and their families and from reports published by the International Red Cross, as well as other sources, 164 persons were victims of forced disappearance in Uruguay. However, of this number 127 disappeared in Argentina and only 32 in Uruguay itself, demonstrating the complicity at work between the security agencies of both countries. A total of 4,933 persons were prosecuted between 1972 and 1985. Most of them were held at the military prisons of Libertad (for men) and Punta de Rieles (for women). The great majority of them spent long years held under harsh conditions and subject to severe physical and psychological abuse. All suffered some form of illness. Having earlier been arrested and kept for days or weeks in clandestine detention centres such as "Karl 300" or "La Tablada" where they were systematically subjected to torture, most detainees were deemed "ready " for prosecution in military courts and moved to one of the two military prisons.

Having come from several months of interrogation under harsh physical and psychological abuse, prisoners might hope that the worst was over, that when they got to prison, at least they would not be beaten or hooded. But an entrance ceremony at EMR1 was designed to sear into memory what lay ahead. Juan Pablo Mirza describes his arrival at Libertad:

> A director had said, "When a prisoner enters, we want him humbled and made to submit from the beginning". So, when in September-October 1972 we arrived as a group, the thirty of us were piled into an "icebox", a hermetically sealed military truck. We had to go at a run from the truck with our satchels, a row of soldiers waiting for us at either side. A soldier hit us on the heel – each one of us pursued by a soldier – making us run, go up five steps in one jump ... I was only in my underwear. Everything in a hurry. They shaved off my hair, hurried me to a shower with boiling water ... off again running, being hit with the stick on my heels and ass. ...They put me into a cell alone. Other forms of welcome included throwing arrivals handcuffed and hooded from the trucks onto the ground.

The newcomer was made to run with his arm bent at the shoulder and held up by the wrist by a soldier who hooked him with his garrotte. When he fell down he was beaten. Once admitted the prisoner was undressed and inspected in every millimetre of anatomy, inside and out. Then he was shaved and given clothing. Before finally going to his cell, he was kept several days in solitary in The Island, with the excuse that he would have to be classified first.[3]

The test of faith

Under these insidious circumstances, which, because of their universality, affected broad swaths of the Uruguayan population, and as military intimidation and control became increasingly pervasive, the churches, related institutions and their leaders became liable to close surveillance under which their activities were monitored. Indeed, several laypersons, students or professionals, active in both the Protestant evangelical and Catholic communities were harassed or detained. (In one incident, later much quoted and the object of hilarity among ecumenical circles, military agents insisted on being told of the clandestine whereabouts in Uruguay of a certain "Paulo de Tarso"[4], apparently referring to correspondence they had examined related to a well-established church activity of the Protestant evangelical churches.) Many were forced to flee into exile: the Evangelical Methodist Church in Uruguay (IEMU), which is an associate member church of the WCC, as well as ecumenical organizations such as ISAL (Church and Society in Latin America), thus "contributed" outstanding leadership for ecumenical service abroad, due to the attacks and pressure brought to bear upon them by the Uruguayan authorities, notably among them the future General Secretary of the WCC, Pastor Emilio Castro. Nonetheless, these churches and related ecumenical movements remained faithful to their calling and provided spiritual support and badly needed material assistance to families of those affected by repression.

The name of the late Luis E. Odell must be mentioned here. He was an esteemed pioneer in education at the *Instituto Crandon* in Montevideo and one of the principal founders of ISAL and former President of the IEMU, and is remembered for his significant and delicate role in alerting the ecumenical family to developments in Uruguay and for his efforts to alleviate suffering at all levels of society. Already in 1974, and as leader in the IEMU, Odell facilitated the departure of many Uruguayans under persecution to seek refugee status abroad, in cooperation with the United Nations High Commissioner for Refugees as well as the Refugee Services (CICARWS) of the WCC.

It became clear, as the scope and nature of repression became known to the international ecumenical family, that two urgent needs required immediate and simultaneous attention: in the first place, assistance to prisoners (whether still held or having been released) and to their families, with priority being given to those located in poor neighbourhoods and, secondly, informing world opinion and the international community on what was occurring in Uruguay, so as to bring maximum pressure for institutional change and a return to the rule of law.

The WCC thus concentrated on these two objectives. It did so in close coordination with key church leaders in the region. Early on, material and financial assistance was discreetly channelled for families through the effective parish work of persons like Methodist pastors Ademar Oliveira and Oscar Bolioli, as well as through partners such as OAAPEL.[5] Increasingly, however, the relatively fragile position of ecumenical and church institutions in Uruguay (the IEMU was quite exposed in its pastoral ministries and circumscribed by military harassment) meant that a variety of other channels were drawn upon to provide assistance to prisoners and their families.

The other objective was to gather information on what was occurring in Uruguay and to disseminate it in a way which would exert maximum leverage on the military authorities. At one level, information on violations of human rights violations was directed to informing churches as well as governments and intergovernmental institutions, such as those within the UN system or those related to the Organization of American States.

At another level, the WCC saw fit to strengthen the efforts of Uruguayan exile communities living in the Americas and in Europe, as they mobilized for a change in the country and for a restoration of democracy there.

For example, an unprecedented initiative of lawyers and jurists from Argentina, Brazil and France joined Uruguayan colleagues in exile, in 1976, to create the International Secretariat of Jurists for Amnesty and Democracy in Uruguay (SIJAU)[6]. Over a number of years it organized a number of high-profile international conferences and missions to countries contiguous to Uruguay, issued crisp newsletters[7] and made appeals to draw attention to the country and to harness the considerable weight of parliamentarians and politicians in isolating the *de facto* regime. SIJAU cooperated closely with members and staff[8] of the International Commission of Jurists, the respected non-governmental organization based in Geneva, Switzerland, as well as with national Bar Associations[9] in various countries. The WCC invested considerable financial resources in this programme, but did so discreetly, so as to avoid drawing its small associated member churches in Uruguay into open conflict with the authorities. Gradually, SIJAU turned its attention to the restoration of civilian rule. When that occurred, a decision was taken by its members to constitute a similar effort with a focus on Paraguay. It was re-named the International Secretariat for Amnesty and Democracy in Paraguay (SIJADEP), and proved itself to be an effective complementary ally of the social and political forces for change in that country, after General Alfredo Stroessner fled into exile in 1989.

The Return

Ecumenical support for humanitarian assistance developed throughout these years from many quarters worldwide, including the WCC, to enable Uruguayan organizations to meet urgent needs among the population. Always discreet, such work essentially concentrated on the reinsertion of freed prisoners into society and creating work schemes for returning exiles after 1985. Centres were rapidly set up in Montevideo to provide urgent psychiatric and psychological assistance and rehabilitation for former prisoners and other torture victims. These and other programmes enabled former prisoners and returnees to find a new life in Uruguayan society under the umbrella of or related to the Uruguay chapter of the YMCA, such as the Servicio Ecuménico de Reintegración (SER) and the Servicio de Rehabilitación Social (SERSOC), by creating viable self-help work opportunities for thousands of Uruguayans.

An unusual but highly relevant intiative was taken by the Disciples of Christ Church in Argentina to channel assistance to the thirty-one officers of the Uruguayan armed forces who had remained faithful to the Uruguayan constitution, refusing to join the military *coup d'état* and participating in the public protest at the closure of Parliament. They had been imprisoned throughout the entire period of thirteen years of military rule, were singled out for particularly harsh prison treatment and, even after the return to civilian governance, did not benefit from having their previous officers' ranks restored to them. The initiative, accompanied by the WCC, was acted upon through the Argentinian human rights group the Ecumenical Movement for Human Rights (MEDH) and with the judicious complicity of the Uruguayan sociologist, Professor Julio Barreiro, of ISAL. This pioneer of lucid ecumenical leadership, a longtime mentor and friend of the worldwide ecumenical family, died in October 2005. He was an invaluable guide to many friends, including this author, demonstrating how to manoeuvre safely through the political, military and urban labyrinths within both Montevideo and Buenos Aires during the period of repression. Above all, Julio contributed greatly to our understanding of the major background issues of power[10] underpinning *de facto* regimes, while pointing to the signs of hope for the future.

Meanwhile, we worked closely, for example, with COSUR[11], an Amnesty International-related group based in Mexico under the able leadership of the esteemed Uruguayan scholar, Lucía Sala de Touron. It had set up an efficient, fair and water-tight system by which small amounts of (anonymous) financial help were channelled to as many prisoners and their families as possible during the early 1980s. A sincere but touchingly playful letter of thanks from one recipient in Uruguay, was shared with Emilio Castro by Professor Touron[12]

> *Dear Friend: I don't know if you are male or female, nor can I imagine how you found out about our situation. Of course we thank you for having sent this money but we have a lot of questions that we want to ask you to answer as soon as possible. How did you know? We have four children and financial difficulties as well. Did we meet each other at some time and we can't remember it? The cash was very welcome above all in these difficult times ...*

A centre of hope

By that time, SERPAJ-Uruguay had been founded (1981) under the leadership of the Jesuit priest Father Luis Pérez Aguirre, affectionately called Perico,[13] and had become *the* important focal point for a prophetic denunciation of human rights violations in the country. It also provided space and public support for the organization of the families of prisoners and of the Mothers' Committee of the Disappeared.[14] The staff of SERPAJ-Uruguay and its offices immediately came under surveillance and threats of closure by the military. Fr. Aguirre himself was detained and tortured on four different occasions. Responding to appeals from its leadership for international solidarity, the WCC alerted its constituencies and joined many churches, councils and human rights coalitions worldwide in demanding from the Uruguayan authorities that this unique human rights organization in Uruguay be allowed to function.[15]

Both Fr. Aguirre and another priest, Fr. Jorge Osorio, sought and obtained ecumenical assistance, including that of the WCC so that the families of prisoners might organize themselves for survival and to enable persons of modest means to benefit from experienced legal help in defending prisoners. In 1984, a hunger strike begun by these two men, together with Methodist pastor Ademar Oliveira, calling for a "national day of reflection", galvanized the country for weeks, during which time many people, by the hundreds, representing a wide range of social forces including labour unions, students and opposition political parties, joined together in solidarity with them and with the actions of SERPAJ, in peaceful and massive demonstrations of resistance to the military governmental restrictions.

This led, by 1985, to a return to constitutional government and to the accelerated release of political prisoners from both military prisons. Uruguay had retrieved its freedom, along with that of its prisoners. Democratic institutions were again soon restored. However, those responsible for the years of repression were never brought to justice,[16] and the scars among Uruguayans ran deep. Much remained to be done to heal the personal traumas, the socio-economic chasms, the political discredit. The last eloquent words in *Nunca Más* express it well:

> What we have been through not only has remained in a hidden corner of memory but has integrated itself into the persona of Uruguayans. It is part of their being, forever. We should have the courage not to hide that experience in our collective subconscious but to recollect it so that we do not fall again into the trap. Let our youth be alert. Let them never sacrifice their conscience and their memory on the altar of petty interests, whether of party, ideology, or conformism. Let them conserve the profound idea of Right and Justice that they received from the founders of our nation and that comes from the Universal Declaration of Human Rights.[17]

The tragic accidental traffic death of Father Aguirre, in 2001, elicited a wave of grief and tribute from ordinary Uruguayans as well as from hundreds of persons worldwide who had come to respect his sterling personal qualities of modesty and courage, and to honour his enormous contributions to our ecumenical understanding of what it means, as Christians, to defend the right of others for dignity and full life.

NOTES

[1] Movement of National Liberation, MLN.
[2] *Uruguay Nunca Más: Human Rights Violations, 1972-1985*, translated from the Spanish original by Elizabeth Hampsten (Philadelphia,, PA, USA: Temple University Press, 1992), page IX.
[3] *Uruguay Nunca Más, op cit.*, pp. 129-130.
[4] the apostle.
[5] Oficina de Asesoramiento y Administración de Proyectos Ecuménicos Latinamericanos. (Office for Advice and Administration of Latin American Ecumenical Projects).
[6] Secretariado Internacional de Juristas por la Amnistía y la Democracia en Uruguay, (International Secretariat for Jurists for Amnesty and Democracy in Uruguay), with provisional headquarters in Paris.
[7] Such as that, dated August 17, 1983, signed by the Secretary of its Brazilian affiliate, Belisario dos Santos, Jr., calling immediate attention to the raid by police on the headquarters of SERPAJ in Montevideo and appealing for urgent international support for its struggle.
[8] A special mention must be made here to underline the strong contribution to SIJAU by the Uruguayan lawyer, Alejandro Artucio, who was later to play an important role in the work of the UN Sub-Commission on the Prevention of Discrimination and Protection of Minorities on the question of impunity enjoyed by the perpetrators of crimes against humanity.
[9] In Argentina, for example, the Centre for Legal and Social Studies/Centro de Estudios Legales y Sociales (CELS) represented the SIJAU effectively, with vigour and professional acuity.
[10] Such as the nature and scope of the National Security Doctrine.
[11] Comité de Solidaridad con Uruguay.
[12] 25 November 1983.
[13] As the founder of SERPAJ-Uruguay, the late Jesuit priest Luis Pérez Aguirre, remarked in June 1983, that SERPAJ, as a Latin American continent-wide organization, was founded, "paradoxically", in Montevideo at a meeting chaired by Pastor Earl Smith in 1968. Fr. Aguirre was strongly encouraged in 1980 by Nobel Prize winner Adolfo Pérez Esquivel, founder of SERPAJ in Argentina, to reinvigorate Montevideo's chapter.
[14] Readers are encouraged to read the profoundly touching book, *Perdidos en el Bosque*, by Alberto Silva, published in 1989 by the Familiares de Uruguayos Detenidos / Desaparecidos, which contains the personal stories surrounding the fates of the twenty-two Uruguayan children whose parents were detained and made to disappear during the years of repression. It is magnificently – and searingly – illustrated by school sketches drawn by some of the children to describe their experiences.
[15] The Canadian ecumenical coalition, Inter-Church Committee on Human Rights in Latin America, an ecumenical coalition with which the WCC's human rights team enjoyed privileged and fruitful collaboration over the years, was particularly active during the campaign to mobilize church and political support for SERPAJ.
[16] Guillermo Kerber, Luis Pérez Aguirre, Arceli E. de Rocchietti, Carlos Delmonte and Ademar Oliveira examine the profound biblical-theological, ethical, political, social and pastoral issues surrounding the impunity enjoyed by the military regime in Uruguay following the passing of the Amnesty Law of 1986, in *Impunity: An Ethical Perspective: Six case studies from Latin America*, Charles Harper, ed. (Geneva: WCC Publication, 1996), pp 29-58 .
[17] *Ibid.*, pp. 317-318.

4

The Coup
Chile

Coup d'état

Since the terrorist attacks on the World Trade Center twin towers in New York City, "9/11" has symbolized the date of that terrible tragedy in 2001, and subsequently became the reference point of the US Administration's global "War on Terrorism". For many Latin Americans, however, 11 September will forever remind people of that morning more than thirty years ago, in 1973, on which Chilean air force jet fighters strafed *La Moneda,* the presidential palace in Santiago de Chile; the day when, under the orders of US-backed General Augusto Pinochet Ugarte, the army invaded the palace and President Salvador Allende died defending the longest-standing constitutional democracy in the continent.

The *coup d'état* that came on the heels of the military takeover in Uruguay marked the crest of the wave of militarism sweeping across the region for more than a decade. Thousands of Allende supporters were rounded up and placed under military guard in the national stadium in the following days, many of them refugees from other Latin American military dictatorships who had fled to Chile as political exiles. It ushered in a period of repression that led to the deaths of over three thousand Chilean civilians and caused an additional thousand to disappear. It precipitated the forced exodus of thousands of Brazilians, Uruguayans and other Latin Americans who had been granted refugee status in Chile during the late 1960s and early 1970s. Thousands of Chileans also fled into exile in neighbouring Latin American countries and to places as far away as Australia, Israel, Sweden, Switzerland and Canada.

The *coup* took the world by surprise, but Chileans had feared its coming as they experienced increasing social and political polarisation exacerbated by the US Central Intelligence Agency's[1] covert support of right-wing opponents of Allende's socialist government during the three years following his election. It ushered in a period of massive violations of human rights by the State on a scale without precedent[2] since Chile gained independence from Spain in 1818.[3] Official terror followed closely and built upon the Brazilian model, characterized by abuse of power, persecution, internal banishment, detention without charge, torture, forced disappearances, executions, and outright killings at the hands of the police, the military and other government agents.

Pinochet's harsh rule lasted until 1990, when, two years after he was defeated in a popular referendum organized to keep his regime in office,[4] he was forced to cede power. On 11 March 1990 the newly elected president of Chile, Patricio Aylwin, the successful candidate of the Christian Democrat Party, was inaugurated.

The sombre figure of the General has become a notorious global symbol of dictatorial disdain, of corruption and of the impunity enjoyed by the perpetrators of gross human rights violations. The truth of the terrible legacy of the military establishment and its security apparatus instituted by him is now, thirty years later, well known and widely substantiated[5]. Pinochet was finally arrested and charged with crimes against named individuals in London on 16 October 1998, on order of the Spanish judge Balthazar Garzón. Though he was subsequently released by the UK on "humanitarian" grounds and returned to Chile his detention became a "transformational moment for the human rights movement"[6]. The wide media coverage which ensued guaranteed that henceforth the name of the Chilean leader will forever be universally associated with crimes against humanity, and in the human collective memory as a symbol of inhumanity.

Soon after he took office, President Aylwin set into motion a process by which the full scope and nature of human rights violations which occurred during the seventeen years of Pinochet rule, were documented. Early on he appointed a Chilean National Commission on Truth and Reconciliation[7], whose members and staff compiled a mammoth and detailed Report[8] based on the recorded personal testimony of family members of victims and information received from many sources, including the churches in Chile. Its sober findings and analysis of this period, its naming of the institutions responsible for crimes, and its sensitivity to the victims and their families, make this Report a main reference for present and future "Truth and Reconciliation" commission (TRC, or "Never Again") investigations subsequently undertaken in other countries around the world that have experienced similar tragedies.

The Report stated:

Very soon after September 11, 1973, the armed forces and police accomplished their most immediate objective, to bring the country under their control and to eliminate any pockets of armed resistance on the part of supporters of the deposed regime. Such resistance can truly be said to have been minimal.[9] Arrests took place in a variety of ways. In some cases particular people were ordered to report to the military authorities, either in general or to a specific place. When they complied with this request they were arrested. Some arrests occurred when a particular person was sought in his or her house or workplace. ... Roundups became routine in the countryside, and raids were common in the large factories in major cities and in the chief mining areas. In Santiago the more important shantytowns suffered large scale arrests ... These arrests were made throughout the whole country. In the smallest towns the police arrested mayors and aldermen, local political party leaders and everyone they regarded as an "agitator". In major cities thousands of people were arrested.[10] Newspaper accounts, the many eyewitness reports the Commission heard, and the reports of the armed forces themselves all indicate just how massive these operations were ... Prisoners were transferred to detention sites. Some people were taken from there and executed, and their dead bodies were left on major streets throughout the city of Santiago and its environs. There were particularly large numbers of bodies left in places like the General San Martin Highway heading towards Los Andes, the road to Valparaiso near the Lo Prado Tunnel, and the intersection of Americo Vespucio and Avenida Grecia, the Metropolitan Cemetery and elsewhere.[11]

Torture of prisoners was common practice during this period, primarily during the interrogation sessions to which they were subjected in almost all detention sites in the Region. Beatings, abuse, and other inhuman and degrading treatment of prisoners were also common procedure. The National Stadium was prepared on September 12 and 13, and it then became by far the largest detention site in this region with more than seven thousand detainees by September 22 according to the International Red Cross. Between two and three hundred of these were foreigners from a variety of nations.[12]

On the night of October 20, 1973, the following persons were executed: José Tomás Beltran Bizama, 25, a worker, Eduardo Antonio Fonseca Castro, 26, a street vendor, and Hernán Anselmo Cortes Velasquez, 22, a worker: none of whom were politically active. In the presence of witnesses a police patrol that was moving about in an ambulance arrested all three of them in their homes in the 18 de Septiembre squatter settlement near the central railroad station and took them away. The next morning their bodies were found in an empty lot along the Lo Errazuriz road in the Maipú district. According to the autopsy reports, the cause of death was multiple perforating bullet wounds to the head.[13]

The two volumes of the Commission's Report, totalling 907 pages in length, contain eyewitness testimonies that illustrate the 2,279 cases of the persons killed or forcibly disappeared that the commission's staff examined.

> They shot him on the road near our house. I heard the shots, and I came out and found his body. They yelled at me to go bury the dog that had just been killed. That dog was my only son. They gave me three hours to bury him and get out of town. I had to wrap him in a blanket, get an oxcart, and leave him in the cemetery.[14]
>
> I had searched for him so much. I went down to the beach to cry, and there he was, all swollen with bullet wounds. They had pulled out his teeth.[15]
>
> When they took my father, they took my husband and me as well. I was raped by a whole group that was guarding me. I never told my husband. That was fifteen years ago.[16]
>
> On windy nights, my mother thought the creak in the door was him. She used to get up to let him in, and then she would weep.[17]
>
> My daughter doesn't talk to me about this issue. I know she's doing it to avoid causing me problems, but she's writing a diary. I've read it, and it's filled with bitterness.[18]
>
> This is the first time we've made a formal accusation. We were afraid, and we didn't have money for the fare.[19]

Chilean and other Latin American ecumenical representatives foresaw the new threats of military intervention in the region at an early consultation which took place in San Juan, Puerto Rico, 23-28 February 1973, seven months before the Chilean coup d'état. Organized by the Commission of the Churches on International Affairs of the WCC, the report of the consultation, entitled *Derechos Humanos y Las Iglesias en America Latina*[20] drew a desolate picture of brutal repression already sweeping across the region and warned the international community of the "ever greater number of people persecuted or made refugees or prisoners for their political views". It called urgently upon the churches in Latin America and worldwide to engage in energetic efforts to make their constituencies aware of these dangers. This far-sighted group of Latin American delegates went further, urging the churches and the WCC to create ecumenical instruments for the implementation of human rights.

The 1973 September 11, military take-over in Chile brought an immediate ecumenical response, as the churches there, caught in the violence of the early days, became only too aware of what was happening and who was affected. Information was rapidly transmitted to the WCC and a stream of consultations ensued with churches and ecumenical partners in Argentina and Peru, soon recognized as places of immediate refuge for those targeted for repression by the new military régime. Communication with Chile was difficult, even hazardous. Soon after the coup, the WCC delegated two trusted and experienced ecumenical veterans, Mrs. Annie Went, Director of the Dutch Interchurch Agency for Refugees, and Dr. Theo Tschuy, the Swiss former Secretary of WCC's Latin America Desk of CICARWS, on a fact-finding mission to Santiago de Chile, Buenos Aires, and Lima. Their assessments of the general situation confirmed the darkest portrayals thus far received outside Chile ("Santiago looks like an occupied city...helicopters cruise above us at frequent intervals ...on-the-spot executions during the curfew hours at night..."). Despite the dangers, they met and conferred with most of the church leaders, UN personnel and other non-church organizations on site.

The practical recommendations made by the two delegates resulting from this first outside ecumenical visit after 11 September, established new vital links of cooperation and solidarity and strengthened existing ones between the churches and ecumenical organizations in Chile and the ecumenical family abroad through the WCC. The most urgent task was to protect foreign nationals, who had sought safe haven in Chile from other South American military dictatorships. Formal agreements were needed to allow them entry to Argentina and Peru, and the WCC provided ecumenical coordination with the Buenos Aires office of the UN High Commissioner for Refugees (UNHCR) that led to the creation of the *Comisión Argentina de Refugiados* (CAREF) with its strong representation from the Protestant Evangelical and Orthodox communities. In the same spirit, the regional ecumenical organization, the *Comisión Evangélica Latinoamericana de Educación Cristiana* (CELADEC), with headquarters in Lima, oversaw the entry of refugees into Peru. By December 1973 the WCC had created the Chile Emergency Desk[21] to accompany and stimulate these efforts. (The Latin American Council of Churches (CLAI) had not yet come into existence.[22])

CONAR

In Chile, the first of the five church-related organizations[23] created to respond to the emergency situation, and that later developed strong programmes of social and juridical assistance and rehabilitation, was formed: the National Committee of Refugees (CONAR), headed by Bishop Helmut Frenz, of the Evangelical Lutheran Church in Chile, a member church of the WCC; and representatives of several other churches, such as Mr. José Elías Aboid, the Apostolic Administrator of the Catholic Orthodox Church; Monseñor Sergio Correa, of the Roman Catholic Church; Pastor Augusto Fernandez Arlt, representative of the regional ecumenical body UNELAM *(Comisión Provisional Pro Unidad Evangélica Latinoamericana);* Samuel Nalegash, a member of the Methodist Pentecostal Church, as its Executive Secretary. With a daunting task of assisting foreigners to leave Chile under protection, representatives from CONAR and the representative of the UNHCR, Oldrich Haselman, reached a rapid agreement with Gen. Augusto Pinochet's new military government. The speed at which it was achieved, according to the delegation's confidential report, "can only be explained by the latter's overriding desire to rid Chile of all foreign 'leftist extremists', to use their own terminology. Through this programme, some five thousand foreigners who had sought refuge in Chile under Salvador Allende's elected government were able to depart safely from Chile to other destinations.

During the next months, an increasing number of Chileans, individually or in families, also fled to neighbouring countries. The capacity of the Argentine state-run services to receive them, as well as that of other countries, was soon overwhelmed. It became imperative that churches and other groups be equipped to assist them in practical ways. With the encouragement and help of the UNHCR, the above-mentioned ecumenical group, CAREF, as well as many church communities and ecumenical organizations in Mendoza (just across the border from Chile) and Buenos Aires took the lead in providing protection, food and shelter for hundreds of exiles.

The critical situation in Chile, the heavy burden this entailed for churches in the region and the need for further on-the-spot information led the WCC to send another, three-person, delegation – headed by the Rev. John H. Sinclair, of the United Presbyterian Church (USA); together with Ms. Margareta Grape-Lanz from the Church of Sweden; and Pastor Julio Amaral, representing the French ecumenical service agency, CIMADE – to visit the churches in Santiago, Buenos Aires and Lima. This delegation provided the Council with valuable insights into the situation and, on the basis of its productive and sometimes tense dialogues with the churches and ecumenical groups in these capitals, it recommended priorities for action in response to the evolving Chilean crisis and gave timely advice on which channels were best suited to implement them.

COPACHI

One of those urgent priorities was to mobilize support for another initiative within Chile: to protect persecuted Chileans. Hundreds were seeking help from the churches, particularly from the Roman Catholic archdiocese. On 6 October 1973 the Committee of Cooperation for Peace in Chile (popularly known as the *Comité Pro Paz*, or COPACHI) was established under the ecclesiastical authority of Cardinal Raúl Silva Henríquez, the Roman Catholic Archbishop of Santiago. He was convinced that the churches should "take care of Chileans who may be in grave economic or personal necessity as a result of recent political events"[24]. On his initiative and with the full cooperation of Lutheran Bishop Helmut Frenz, a widely ecumenical governing board was set up to guide the work of the Committee. Under the strong leadership of co-presidents Frenz and the Roman Catholic Bishop Fernando Ariztia, with participation of the Evangelical Lutheran, Methodist, Pentecostal, and Orthodox churches, and the Jewish community, the Committee ably oversaw the work of a committed group of lawyers, social workers, health workers and other volunteers who dared to undertake the challenge, one which demanded unprecedented efficiency, sensitivity and courage. It appointed Father Fernando Salas, SJ, to direct the work of the Committee, which he did with panache. During its brief, two-year tenure, COPACHI'S staff and supporters in Chile received hundreds of ordinary citizens – people who had been subject to raids, searches, detention, torture and other forms of repression, for the most part in the poor and working class neighbourhoods. For this, they were constantly harassed and intimidated by agents of the military regime.

A grim and potentially damaging incident, yet with its moments of humour, occurred at 8.00 p.m. on 15 May, 1975. The building in which COPACHI and one of its programmes, *Comsode*, were housed was surrounded by soldiers and agents of the DINA (secret police headed by the infamous Manuel Contreras Sepúlveda). Two hours earlier a young man, a leader in the Socialist Party, Sergio Jaime Zamora Herrera – who had earlier been tortured – had escaped from a DINA vehicle and dashed through Comsode's front door at 2216 Calle Santa Mónica, with two Dina agents in hot pursuit. It was already dark outside and the staff was winding up its work. Storming up the staircase after Zamora, the agents with drawn pistols started grabbing him and yelling. Staff – men and women – poured out of their offices and spontaneously surrounded Zamora and the agents, shouting: "This is the house of the Archbishop ...the Cardinal!". *"Mierda!"*, exclaimed one of the agents, "This is the *Comité!*" and they rushed down the stairway and into the street to call for reinforcements by radio transmitter. Zamora was whisked out of the building, examined by a trusted physician and given protection.

One of the staff alerted the Cardinal, others phoned board members and staff who had already gone home, warning of an impending raid and crisis. Other telephone calls were made by board members to the US Ambassador and to the Chief Justice of the Supreme Court, urging them to secure from General Pinochet a guarantee that no raid would be made. Ecumenical unity had never been so clear. The word spread: "Get down here and show yourself!" From all over the city, Protestant pastors and Catholic priests rushed to put on clerical collars (some, unused to wearing them in a modern society, scrambled into backroom trunks and cartons for seminary-day vestiges). Crosses of venerable or less venerable origin, in impressive or discreet shapes and sizes draped the necks of lay people and clergy alike. By the time this battalion of "clergy" arrived from both ends of *Calle Santa Mónica*, DINA agents and police were everywhere, waiting for orders to go in and take Zamora by force. Their astonishment and irritation was palpable as dozens of men of the cloth walked calmy through their midst. It was an electric moment. Slowly, the members of COPACHI/COMODE emerged from the building to go home. As they did each man or woman was surrounded and accompanied by four or five members of the religious community for protection. (The author, on a staff visit from Geneva precisely that week, was assigned to "sit by the phone" in the hotel where he was staying, just in case things became ugly and international friends needed to be informed). By midnight, the small crisis committee of Copachi had been set up, arranged to meet emissaries from General Pinochet and informed them that Zamora was being treated elsewhere for proven torture. Finally, all departed and the lights were turned off. The "Cardinal" had won this one.[25]

On 3 October of that year, 1975, Bishop Helmut Frenz, in Geneva for a conference, received news that he had been permanently expelled from Chile. A month later, in November, several senior members of COPACHI, including its director Fr Fernando Salas and José Zalaquett, head of its legal department, were arrested and assigned to the *Tres Alamos* detention centre. Zalaquett was expelled from the country four months later. The COPACHI was closed by an executive order issued by General Pinochet on the last day of December 1975.

Developing ecumenical guidelines

Early on, the WCC had realized that it must respond quickly and energetically to calls for help from member churches and ecumenical friends in Chile and elsewhere in Latin America caught up in this situation of such great stress and need. It stepped up its financial assistance to both committees CONAR and COPACHI, while at the same time – with great restraint – abstaining from issuing public statements strongly critical of General Pinochet's regime, so as to avoid placing its constituency in Chile in still greater jeopardy.

There were exceptions to this rule of restraint, in instances where individuals – particularly active members of the ecumenical movement – were harassed or threatened with exile, detention or worse. In several such instances, direct appeals were often addressed directly to the military authorities so as to warn them of international repercussions should harm come to these persons.[26] Furthermore, our experience in Chile and in other countries, demonstrated that ecumenical intervention on behalf of a person or group identified as being a member of the church community often provided opportunities to intercede on behalf of a wider sector of society and to communicate strong objection to violations affecting classes of threatened persons. This action guideline was reaffirmed in the criteria in a statement adopted by the WCC's Central Committee meeting in 1976, three years after the Chilean coup, that included reference to "situations where a statement may safeguard the lives or physical well-being, or bring effective relief to victims of conflict or injustice"[27].

The wisdom of this early decision was corroborated at the time when the Social Aid Foundation of the Christian Churches (FASIC)[28] came into existence[29] several months before COPACHI was forced to cease its activites and was immediately succeeded by the Vicariate of Solidarity of the Archdiocese of Santiago[30].

The WCC thus adopted a strategic approach to guide its actions towards Chile: in the first place, we closely accompanied the people who directed and worked in these organizations through visible, frequent and regular staff visits to them and the sending of delegations composed of lay and clergy representatives of the worldwide ecumenical constituency and often of sister international non-governmental organizations, such as the International Commission of Jurists. Secondly and simultaneously, we worked quietly to support financially the efforts of Chilean church-related organizations, through appeals for substantial financial grants addressed to member churches and agencies. Thirdly, we sought to make judicious use of the privileged information provided by these and other local sources, so as to channel timely, credible data to WCC-related churches and to a number of governments and parliaments actively opposing the Pinochet regime, and to appropriate UN agencies and regional intergovernmental bodies. The Vicariate of Solidarity was one of the main sources of substantial, precise and systematized information which was surreptitiously ferreted out of Santiago's heavily monitored Pudahuel airport by the occasional visitor, staff member or member of a religious order, to be gratefully received by staff of the WCC and United Nations civil servants.[31]

Vicaría de la Solidaridad

The Vicariate of Solidarity of the Archdiocese of Santiago welcomed in 1976 the Association of Relatives of the Detained-Disappeared into its huge honeycomb of offices in the building adjoining the Roman Catholic Cathedral of Santiago on the *Plaza de Armas*. The Vicariate, admirably headed by Fr. Cristián Precht Bañados, was engaged in the herculean task of providing legal and social assistance to Chileans, and to the collection of data and analysis relating to the repression in the country. The presence of these (mostly) women relatives of victims of forced disappearance in their corridors and at the coffee corner was a constant reminder of the depth of the criminal activity of the *Junta Militar*, of the courageous resistance of ordinary people to it, and, importantly, of the working class background of most of them.

They were to become one of the most effective groups in Chile, and indeed – through the unity and strength represented by its adhesion to the Latin American Federation of Associations of the Relatives of the Disappeared (FEDEFAM) – on the international scene, demanding the truth about their disappeared loved ones, and justice. The leadership of such women as the late Sola Sierra and her successor Viviana Díaz, stands out for its authenticity and courage in engaging in public demonstrations and hunger strikes to make their demands known.[32] They also persistently pressed for the adoption of a United Nations standard and instrument designed to oblige member states of the UN to prevent the forced disappearance of persons. This was obtained, after years of effort of FEDEFAM and other international non-governmental organizations, on 23 September 2005, when the Intersessional Working Group of the Human Rights Commission, meeting in Geneva, adopted the International Convention for the Protection of All Persons from Enforced Disappearance.

The Vicariate organized a major Symposium on Human Rights in November 1978 under the very nose of the regime, and to its great irritation. A considerable number of representatives of the international community – governments, churches and non-governmental organizations – from Latin America and other regions of the world were present. Its theme was "Everyone has the right to be a person". One of the strongest moments came when, on the stage facing these dignitaries, a small group of women danced the *cueca sola*, a traditional and vastly popular courtship ritual performed by Chileans of all ages at feasts and celebrations. The heavy silence of each observer – watching each dancer in gracious steps revolving with colourful kerchief around the empty space where her loved one should have been – spoke volumes about the drama being played out within Chile at that moment. In 1985 an esteemed senior functionary of the *Vicaría*, José Manuel Parada, was brutally murdered by the police, and other staff members were harassed or imprisoned – a high price to pay for fidelity to the imperatives of the Gospel.

There is no doubt that the mammoth work of the *Vicaría* during those sixteen years of its existence became a living symbol of care and of justice in Chile. In the words spoken by Argentine theologian José Míguez Bonino, a president of the WCC who represented it at the Symposium, the *Vicaría* "has been a place of refuge, a sanctuary for all those uprooted by conflict or human injustice".

The *Vicaría* was not the only institution to be criticized by the military regime. General Pinochet attacked the WCC itself by name, accusing it of "fomenting subversion in Chile" by its support for the work of the *Vicaría* and other church-related projects benefitting the victims of repression.[33]

FASIC

The xenophobic Pinochet regime was not only eager to rid Chilean society of all "foreign extremists", it also sought to remove any trace of the Allende period. By 1975 the number of arrests in the country had reached considerable proportions,[34] and many of the persons who had been considered particularly dangerous to the stability of the new regime had been murdered or "disappeared".[35] At the end of the year the protected staging areas, where foreign refugees were allowed to await departure, were practically empty. The thousands (over 9600)[36] of asylum seekers who had taken refuge in foreign embassies immediately after the coup had left for far-flung countries. However, the huge numbers of Chilean prisoners condemned of "crimes" by military courts were suffering great privation, and the churches were particularly sensitive to their needs.

To attend to this challenge, a new ecumenical body, FASIC,[37] was created, presided over by Methodist Bishop Juan Vásquez del Valle, and a vice-president, Roman Catholic Bishop Jorge Hourton. Other members were José Elías Aboid, who had been a member of the board of CONAR; Pastor José Alfredo Ramires, of the Methodist Pentecostal Church; Bishop Esteban Schaller of the Evangelical Lutheran Church, María Loreto Romo representing the staff and Claudio González, its Executive Secretary. Over the years and until the present, membership of the board has been renewed. However, the ecumenical character of FASIC has always been firmly maintained, in spite of some ecclesiastical and political pressures to weaken it. As a result, FASIC is the only national church-related organization in Chile today which has remained faithful to this premise.

Its first task was to assist political prisoners with long sentences to opt for leaving the country to a new life elsewhere. This was made possible by an agreed protocol *(Decreto Supremo No. 504)* signed between the military regime and the Inter-Governmental Committee for European Migration (ICEM). The important underlying premise was that many Chilean men and women would accept this alternative to prison and go into exile. Soon, FASIC developed a programme of personal accompaniment of family members of prisoners who had already left Chile, enabling them to join their loved one in their new adopted places of residence and work in many countries around the world. Churches, the general public and the media in places like Great Britain, New Zealand, France, the Nordic countries, North America and elsewhere became keenly aware of developments in Chile during the past thirty years, very largely thanks to the dynamic presence of organized and motivated communities of Chileans and their families who settled there. They helped maintain the high level of political and church solidarity worldwide, for Chile and Chileans, occasionally overshadowing similar campaigns for Latin America. They organized celebratory or commemorative events in which songs by the revered Chilean folk–singer Victor Jara were sung and the poems of Pablo Neruda recited. Chileans also held dramatic hunger strikes in solidarity with their compatriots at home (including a memorable week-long one staged, paradoxically, at the Ecumenical Centre in Geneva) that nurtured worldwide awareness.

During the 1980s and 1990s, FASIC responded to new needs among the population. When the *Vicaría de la Solidaridad* (the successor of COPACHI) closed down its services in 1992, when a democratic civilian government was put in place, FASIC took over the large load of pending trial dossiers of its legal department. Under the leadership of its experienced legal expert, Verónica Reyna, FASIC arranged visits to prisons, offering legal, material and moral support to men and women who had been tried by military courts and who remained in Chile, and to their families. In 1977, a specialized team of psychologists and psychiatrists *(Equipo Médico Psiquiátrico)*, for the most part women, had initiated indispensable therapeutic work with torture victims. Their in-depth work engendered both seminal theoretical studies and initiated sharing with persons engaged in similar programmes across the region, so vast were the number of victims of torture and their effects identified. Pioneers like psychologist Elisabeth Lire and Fanny Pollarolo, a psychiatrist on the FASIC team, were thus in constant contact with Paz Rojas Baeza, a neuro-psychiatric physician who coordinates the mental health team of the Committee of the Defence of People's Rights (CODEPU), a sister human rights organization based in Santiago.[38]

It made scholarships available for the sons and daughters of men and women who had been victims of forced disappearance, so that they might continue studying. It set aside generous office and meeting space on the grounds of the converted villa it occupies near the centre of Santiago, for the Association of Relatives of the Detained-Disappeared. And then, after 1990 when this became possible, FASIC played a key role in facilitating the return to Chile of many families in exile, *los retornados*, and assisted former prisoners to build new lives in a changed Chilean society.[39] Eliana Rolemberg expressed it well on the thirtieth anniversary of the founding of FASIC, when she evoked, from the perspective of CESE, another sister ecumenical organization in Brazil, the long solidarity record of FASIC:

> It accumulated experiences of ecumenical service during thirty years and was able to guarantee space for a whole set of churches and ecumenical organizations, deepening its understanding of issues, entering into dialogue, articulating its concerns – all within the perspective of solidarity. It is a space that is occupied by peoples' organizations with their untiring search for the disappeared, a space that unites the different groups who were engaged in common

struggles and who brought them to share with each other, always keeping visible on the horizon the utopia of justice.[40]

FASIC is today the only church-related organization still in existence of the four major programmes set up in the early years of the military regime to respond to the critical needs of the Chilean population.

The Pentecostal churches

José Míguez Bonino – an informal companion throughout this narrative – represented the Argentinian churches and the WCC at the inauguration, in March 1990, of the freshly-elected Chilean President Patricio Aylwin. The author was delighted to be with him, a former President of the WCC and friend, throughout a week of dignified formality and rousing celebration at the restoration of democratic civilian rule. In a personal letter, this keen ecumenical observer wrote that

> It is difficult for an Argentinian (as, I imagine, would also be for a Brazilian or an Uruguayan) to avoid looking at the Chilean transition without using the lenses of our own experience. (...) The difference I see there is that, first, the Catholic Church was involved and, second, that Pentecostal churches were also present – that is, churches which have an insertion at the base of society. Consequently, it is easy to see that human rights organisms seem to have taken root and find expression at that level of society. We saw that in the public demonstrations of these days, where the 'poblaciones' were in a clear majority, there was a festive mood reflecting quite clearly the characteristics of popular culture.[41]

The role and presence of the Pentecostal communities in Chile is, indeed, strong. Right from the start, under military rule, the late Bishop Enrique Chávez, president of WCC's member church, the *Iglesia Pentecostal de Chile*[42] informed delegates at the Fifth Assembly of the WCC meeting in Nairobi, Kenya (1975) – quite courageously, given the policies of the military regime with regard to those who were seen to speak ill of it outside the country. He witnessed to the scale and ferocity of repression affecting the Pentecostal constituency and the Chilean poor majorities in general. It was no coincidence, as the majority of the faithful are people of modest means – workers, miners, families living in isolated communities of the south or in the urban *poblaciones*. As the full analysis of the record of violations of human rights shows, according to the National Commission on Truth and Reconciliation, most of the victims of detention, disappearance, torture, or execution were workers and peasants, from 20 to 35 years of age, and married with children[43], that is, from among the population which constitutes the backbone of Pentecostal communities. It followed that their church leaders – men and women – spoke with unquestionable authority and were among the first to address the needs of the people during this terrible period of political violence. As early as the 1970s, the Misión Iglesia Pentecostal had taken creative initiatives, through its Comisión Técnica Asesora, in a programme of social action[44] carried out in conditions of sharp military repression.

One of the instruments which the Pentecostal Church of Chile created to meet some of those basic needs was the *Servicio Evangélico de Desarrollo*, (SEPADE)[45], which accompanied families concentrated in shantytowns and marginalized regions of the capital and in rural areas where, in fact, most of the Pentecostal churches were to be found. Its programme of popular education emphasising social awareness, led to a strengthening of local social organizations designed to combat poverty, train new leadership in labour unions and in the countryside. Simultaneously, SEPADE invested in building and strengthening a new Christian community (*"una Iglesia popular"*) sensitive to the realities around it as an expression of faith.

The Christian Confraternity of Churches (CCC)[46]

The Pentecostal presence was felt strongly within the *Confraternidad de las Iglesias Cristianas de Chile* (CCC), a body formed in the 1980s and which represents most of the ecumenically and justice-oriented Chilean Protestant churches.[47] On the invitation of the *Confraternidad*, a delegation of the WCC visited Chile in late 1986, to express "solidarity with the churches in Chile in the situation of the state of siege under which they are presently living."[48] In it, the delegation highlighted the "dismal" human rights situation prevailing in the country, especially after the imposition of a state of siege during the previous month. Raids by security forces in the poor neighbourhoods were constant and vicious.

It was within this context that a letter addressed by leaders of the Confraternity to "General Augusto Pinochet Ugarte, President of the Republic of Chile", stands out for its candor and lucidity. It grew out of the efforts of a month of prayer among the member churches of the *Confraternidad*, carried out under the theme, "For Life, Peace and Reconciliation". It was signed by the leaders of seven Protestant churches and the officers of the *Confraternidad*, and delivered personally by Juan Sepúlveda, its General Secretary, with a delegation of its signatories to the *Moneda* presidential palace on 29 August 1986.

Several excerpts are quoted here:

> Dear Mr. President,
>
> Following a period of much prayer and reflection, we, the undersigned, decided to prepare this open letter so you would know how we feel about the grievous situation in our country. We write you as pastors who are moved by our responsibility to protect the lives of all of God's people. We speak for the members of our churches who are overwhelmed by the great difficulties they face and who expect a word from their pastors.
>
> 1. The majority of our urban and rural churches are located in the poorest sectors ... The words – hunger, unemployment, malnutrition, disease, crowding, truancy – are those that most accurately describe the dramatic reality of the Chilean masses. ... We don't have to be economists or work with statistics to see the discrepancies between the sad reality of this country and the rosy picture projected by the government television news channel and official figures. In the light of our Christian faith, this situation is a scandal.
>
> 2. Naturally, the situation just described breeds widespread discontent. In this country there are no legal or respectable channels for expressing discontent and demanding solutions. ... The people turn to the churches which attempt to help out. ... These efforts are not the prime function of the churches but of the State, and they fall far short. ... This situation is totally contrary to the will of God.
>
> 3. Due to the lack of normal channels of social and political participation, the sectors most affected by the situation in the country have chosen alternative forms of expression of their discontent. They see organized protests and strikes as non-violent means of constructive criticism. ... We as Christians recognize them as ethically legitimate. ... We affirm that the charges filed against these leaders are unjust.
>
> 4. With sadness we have observed on many occasions that your Government, instead of trying to hear and understand the reasons for popular discontent, has incomprehensibly concentrated all its efforts to ignore, inhibit, divert and repress all public manifestations. ... In the light of the Holy Scriptures these deeds are unacceptable.
>
> 5. Since the protests began in 1993, the situation of human rights in Chile has deteriorated perceptibly. To the long list of serious situations ...there have been added other crimes that have horrified national and international public opinion. ... It is inconceivable that these deeds are not clarified.
>
> 6. As pastors, we are greatly concerned that your Government is more interested in its public image than in solving the real problems of the country. ... In our opinion, the image of a country is reflected in the life of its people.
>
> 7. All these acts we have described, whose central elements are a great popular discontent and a lack of political will of the government to take this discontent seriously, has produced a veritable climate of war in the country. Today the possibility of dramatic intensification of violence and armed confrontation ... is not far off.

8. The spiral of violence cannot be stopped by more violence. ... Consequently we make a strong, urgent call to the government over which you preside, to act out of generosity and love for the country by immediately beginning a process of transition to democracy that the Chilean people themselves determine through their various organizations. ...

May God give you the necessary wisdom in this moment to accede to this call.
We greet you respectfully,
(the Signatories)[49]

NOTES

[1] Only a year later, in an open letter dated 20 September 1974 to the United States Congress, representatives of mainline Protestant churches in the US vigorously protested at this involvement when it "learned from numerous press accounts and statements by President Gerald Ford that U.S. government agencies were directly involved in a relentless and ultimately successful scheme to bring the popularly elected government of President Salvador Allende of Chile, to an end".

[2] Roman Catholic Bishop Carlos Camus wrote, years later that "we had difficulties getting used to the idea that we began to live a long and cruel dictatorship, which we had never thought possible in Chile. We believed that Chileans did not know how to hate so profoundly, that vengeance has its limits, that our middle class were imbued with a moral sense which was incompatible with torture and sexual aberrations, that the Armed Forces were professionals, respectful of a Christian tradition and that they did not know how to brazenly lie."
(*Represión Política y Defensa de los Derechos Humanos* by Hugo Frühling (ed) (Ediciones Chile-América, 1986), p. 54, as quoted in *Para una Historia de los DD.HH.en Chile: Historia Institucional de la Fundación de Ayuda Social de las Iglesias Cristianas FASIC* 1975-1991, by Mario Garcés and Nancy Nicholls (Santiago: LOM Ediciones/ FASIC, 2005) p. 23

[3] Since the "pacification" of the native Araucanian indigenous population in the late 19th century.

[4] "*ADIÓS GENERAL !!*" reads one of the most sought-after vintage referendum campaign buttons.

[5] Among other locations, in the records of the archives of the US State Department and Congress. See, in this regard, the thorough investigation of unclassified government documents recorded and published by the Washington, DC–based National Security Archives, *The Pinochet File*, by Peter Kornbluh. In it, the author meticulously documents the complicity of the United States administration, and in particular of the US president, Richard Nixon, his secretary of state, Henry Kissinger and the CIA, in the covert preparation and execution of the military coup of September 11th.

[6] Ibid, *op. cit.*, p. xii.

[7] Presided over by Senator Raúl Rettig Guissen.

[8] *Informe de la Comisión Nacional de Verdad y Reconciliación: Texto oficial completo*, initially published in *La Nación, March 5-6, 1991*. Translated by Phillip E. Berryman in *Report of the Chilean National Commission on Truth and Reconciliation* . Introduction by José Zalaquett (Notre Dame, Indiana, USA and London, England: Center for Civil and Human Rights, Notre Dame Law School, University of Notre Dame Press, 1993).

[9] Op. cit., p. 129.

[10] Ibid., p. 132.

[11] Ibid., p. 149.

[12] Ibid., pp. 150-151.

[13] Ibid., p. 227.

[14] Ibid., p. 780.

[15] Ibid., p. 782.

[16] Ibid., p. 782.

[17] Ibid., p. 783.

[18] Ibid., p. 786.

[19] Ibid., p. 792.

[20] Its confidential report, translated from the Spanish by the (then) CCIA staff member who organized the meeting, Dwain C. Epps, is entitled "Consultation on Human Rights and the Churches in Latin America" and is available in the WCC Archives.

[21] In 1975 the Desk was subsumed into the Human Rights Resources Office for Latin America, a programme of WCC's Unit II on Peace, Justice and the Integrity of Creation. It operated from 1975 to 1990.

[22] It was formally constituted in 1982, in Huampani, Peru.

[23] The Comité Nacional de Refugiados (CONAR, 1973-1975); the Comité por la Cooperación por la Paz en Chile (COPACHI, 1973-1975); the Fundación de Acción Social de las Iglesias Cristianas (FASIC, 1975 to the present); the Vicaria de la Solidaridad del Arzobispado de Santiago (VICSOL, 1976-1990) And the Servicio Evangélico pro Desarrollo (SEPADE, 1980 to the present).

[24] Report of the Chilean National Commission, op. cit., p. 463.

[25] A full account of this incident is found in *Chile: La Memoria Prohibida, Vols I-III*, by Eugenio Ahumada, Rodrigo Atria, Javier-Luis Egaña, Augusto Góngora, Carmen Quesney, Gustavo Saball and Gustavo Villalobos (Santiago: Pehuén Editores, 1989), cf Vol. II, pp.91-99.

[26] Such as when Bishop Frenz was permanently prevented by the military authorities from returning to assume his duties in Chile in 1975, after a visit to Europe. Or when an appeal was made directly to the Chilean authorities by WCC's 5th Assembly in Nairobi, calling for the release of imprisoned personnel and members of the Committee for Peace. (*The Churches in International Affairs: Reports 1974-1978*, pp.193 and 188, respectively.)

[27] "The Role of the World Council of Churches in International Affairs". (WCC/CCIA: Reprinted in August 1999), p. 26.

[28] Social Assistance Foundation of Christian Churches, Fundación de Ayuda Social de las Iglesias Cristianas

[29] 12 April 1975.

[30] 1 January 1976.

[31] For an extended period of time in the late 1970s the systematic flow of credible information and substantiated statistical data provided confidentially via couriers or by discreet visits by lawyers of the Vicariate of Solidarity, to the Division (later, Center) of Human Rights of the United Nations, in Geneva, was alleged to constitute sixty to seventy-five per cent of its basic working material in preparation, among other concerns, for the annual consideration of the situation in Chile on the agenda (Item 5) of the Commission on Human Rights.

[32] In 1995, when the Agrupación had been welcomed to set up its headquarters in the offices of FASIC, the entire leadership also included: Mireya Garcia R., Laura Atencio A., Gonzalo Muñoz O. Mariana Guzmán N. and Amanda González del V.

[33] Expreso (Lima: 24 November 1977).

[34] "In May 1975, the Ministry of the Interior acknowledged that there were 41,359 persons detained under the state of emergency".
"En Mayo de 1975, el Ministerio del Interior reconoció que en Chile había 41,359 personas detenidas por estado de sitio." (*La Represión Politica en Chile: los hechos*, by María Eugenia Rojas, p.256).

[35] Garcés, Nicholls, op. cit., p.21.

[36] Idem, p.19.

[37] see xxiii above.

[38] See the article by Dr. Baeza, entitled "Breaking the Human Link: the Medico-Psychiatric View of Impunity", in *Impunity: an Ethical Perspective* (Charles Harper, ed.), Op. cit., pages 73-95.

[39] See the summary of FASIC's impact in the introduction to the excellent institutional history of FASIC, published recently, by Mario Garcés and Nancy Nicholls, *(Para una Historia de los DD.HH. en Chile)*, Op. cit., p.13.

[40] Garcés, Nicholls, op. cit., p .276.

[41] Letter to the author dated 1990 March 13.

[42] Pentecostal Church of Chile. The Misión Iglesia Pentecostal (Pentecostal Mission Church) is also a member church of the WCC in Chile, both of which maintain significant pastoral presence and social projects in the marginalized sectors and neighbourhoods of the country.

[43] Report of the NCTR, op. cit., pp 900-904.

[44] under the direction of Daniel Palma S.

[45] The Protestant Development Service.

[46] *La Confraternidad Cristiana de Iglesias.*

[47] They were, in 1995: *Misión Iglesia Pentecostal; Iglesia de Misiones Pentecostales Libres; Iglesia Wesleyana Nacional; Iglesia Evangélica Luterana en Chile; Iglesia Misión Apostólica Universal; Iglesia Misión Comunión de los Hermanos; Iglesia Evangélica Reformada; Iglesia Pentecostal de Chile; Iglesia Eben Ezer Pentecostal.*

[48] Report of the World Council of Churches Delegation to Chile (28 October-2 November 1986) – translated into English and French from the original Spanish.

[49] Bishop Enrique Chávez C., Pentecostal Church of Chile; Dr. Jorge Cárdenas B., Moderator of the Evangelical Presbyterian Church; Bishop José Flores, Comunión of the Brethren Church; Pastor Edgardo Toro, Director of the National Wesleyan Church; Bishop Sinforiano Gutiérrez, of the Free Pentecostal Missions; Pastor Narciso Sepúlveda, President of the Mission Pentecostal Church; Pastora Juana Albornoz, of the Apostolic Universal Mission Church and Bishop Isaías Gutiérrez, of the Methodst Church in Chile.

5

The Horror
Argentina

The ecumenical efforts in Argentina to protect Chilean refugees, a decade and a half earlier, in 1974, were experiencing serious problems in protecting them. The number of 3,500 Chileans under the protection of the UNHCR, housed in small hotels and homes in Buenos Aires was far surpassed, as repression intensified in Chile, by an estimated 10,000 more Chileans who fled across the high Andean border into Mendoza and other border cities and towns.[1] Under the able leadership of Methodist Pastor Emilio Monti, CAREF[2] vigorously sought to find employment-generating solutions and solutions for the many other problems facing their "guests". Tension was mounting as well in the Chilean community – shared by the churches working with it – because of serious threats to their physical integrity, emanating from political allies and elements within the Argentine armed forces who were favourable to the Pinochet regime. For example, the former Chilean Commander-in-Chief of the Armed Forces under Salvador Allende, Carlos Prats González, was murdered with his wife in the centre of Buenos Aires, by a bomb placed in his automobile by an agent of the notorious secret police, DINA. He had taken refuge there, fearing for his life in Santiago a year before. This caused great consternation in Chile and in Argentina, particularly because it indicated operational complicity with the Argentinian security forces.[3]

The CAREF team in Mendoza, alongside the Ecumenical Foundation of Cuyo (Fundación Ecuménica de Cuyo, or FEC) and the Ecumenical Popular Action (Acción Popular Ecuménica, APE)[4] were on the front line of the flow of entering refugees and experienced similar difficulties, with the added constraints of being at a great distance from the capital, where national decisions were made. Philip Potter, the General Secretary of the WCC, in a move coordinated by CAREF and with sister international agencies, expressed serious concern about these developments to the (then) President of the Republic, Maria Estela Martinez de Perón, in a letter dated 18 November 1974, in which he also urged the government to maintain and open additional facilities for refugees who had been granted political asylum.

A bit of history

It must be remembered that Isabel Perón (called *Isabelita*), had been the third wife of Juan Perón, a colonel who had taken power during the Second World War, was elected in 1946 and became immensely popular with the Argentine people mainly because of the electric appeal of his first wife, Evita, among the poor. After a carefully nurtured exile in 1955 in Spain, he appointed a delegated candidate, Héctor Cámpora, to run for presidential election to prepare his return. Cámpora won, on 25 May 1973, but was almost immediately forced to resign by his chief in Spain, who then returned in triumph on 20 June to a violently divided political landscape, in which rival factions of the right and left among his *Peronista* followers bitterly contested Perón's favour. By the time he died of a heart attack on 1 July 1974, and *Isabelita* had been sworn in as the head of government, facing armed acts of violence from movements of the left and reactions of the extreme right, Argentina was on its way to becoming ripe for practices of State military terror.

> She was as incompetent to check the different terrorist groups as she was to control the terrifying inflation, which had reached an annual rate of 700 percent, or to halt a severe economic decline that had produced a negative growth rate. On 26 March 1976, the military took control yet again … forming a three-man junta. (She) was quietly flown out of Buenos Aires, and after some years of house arrest, back to a Spanish exile.[5]

On 9 September 1975 we received in the Council a monitored telex from Emilio Monti and Alieda Verhoeven, informing us, wisely quoting *La Nación*, that a bomb had exploded on (early) Sunday the 7th in a *"templo de Mendoza"* that is, the parish church of the Evangelical Methodist Church. "Damage was serious to the main entry and to the adjacent buildings", it went on, "but there were no victims". It was an extremely good thing that there were not, since the pastor of that Methodist parish living in the "adjacent building", was Methodist Pastor Federico Pagura, his wife Rita and their family. "It was like a tremendous earthquake", she is quoted as saying. Although the perpetrators of the attack were never identified, there was a strong suspicion that the attack was carried out because of the solidarity work which Pastor

Pagura and the ecumenical community in Mendoza was carrying out among Chilean refugees. Many messages of solidarity followed from Argentine and other churches and councils, and soon ecumenical resources were found to repair the damage. Reinforcements came for the protection and public support for the work of the specialized teams under the auspices of the UNHCR, the WCC and the *Comisión Coordinadora de Acción Social (Católico-Protestante)* among the Chilean refugees and migrants. The Argentine military coup d'état of 24 March 1976 was only six months distant. The abduction of Professor Mauricio López, the esteemed colleague of the ecumenical team in Mendoza, was only fifteen months away.

MEDH

A predecessor of sorts of the Ecumenical Movement for Human Rights (MEDH), began its existence in 1975, with three people concerned deeply about the suffering of persons around them. As was the case in many instances throughout this period in Latin America, individuals came together to do something to help others in a critical situation. Others joined them. They shared information and organized their time and allotted tasks. Outside resources were low or non-existent. They worked out of vulnerable work places or from their own modest living quarters. Soon they sought institutional help – and eventually became a vibrant member of "civil society". Jorge Correa and Jorge and Nelly Pascale helped some of the first persons affected by the violence, families of the disappeared. They assisted ordinary Argentinians in urgent need of legal assistance, as well as finding ways of fleeing the country. Simultaneously an embryonic *Comissión de Familiares*, with the help of some pastors, was meeting discreetly in the basement of a Protestant evangelical church, since there were well-founded fears, according to one jurist, that some were targeted by the AAA.[6]

It was an extremely tense period. The conflict between armed left guerrillas and the police left civilians vulnerable to detention, not to mention stray bullets. Security agents proliferated. It was a time when a Methodist lawyer made appointments with family members, so as to prepare to initiate procedures of *habeas corpus* on behalf of a disappeared relative, at a certain street corner within a specific ten-minute span. If one or the other did not appear, they had to go through the whole contact scheduling once again.

This initial work by commited individuals was soon strengthened by the human and institutional resources of the churches working together. A veritable movement of leaders and lay people of the churches came together to discuss the emergency situation in 1975 and to decide what actions to take in order to meet the needs of the most affected. Thus, on 19 March 1976, the *Movimiento Ecuménico de los Derechos Humanos* (MEDH)[7] came into being, five days before the coup by the military Junta. Pastor José de Luca tells of how Argentines had been warned and taught to be ready for the repression which was coming, by the very fact that Argentina had taken into its midst during the previous three years the Uruguayan and Chilean refugees, who became, in a real sense, their mentors.[8] The movement's fundamental biblical and ethical principles were published in July of that year, in a historic document,[9] for it articulated the sharp sense of unity among the churches committed to human rights. Several, but not all, were there: Protestant evangelical churches and those few Catholic dioceses which were ready to work together in a risky but necessary ministry of both pastoral and prophetic import within Argentine society on the cusp of a slope plunging it into a seven-year period of unprecedented horror.

In December, a large public gathering took place in the Catholic cathedral of Quilmes. The names of some of MEDH's first leaders evoke respect and esteem: Catholic Bishop Jorge Novak, of Quilmes; Bishop Federico Pagura, Pastors Van der Velde (Refomed Church), Guillermo Arming (Evangelical Church of the River Plate), Enrique A. Lavigne (Methodist) and Gabriel Vaccaro (Pentecostal); Sra. Blanca S. de Martínez (Disciples of Christ); Dr. Frugoni Rey (Legal Assessor); Fathers Mario Leonfanti and José Andrés (Catholic). Throughout the history of this vast ecumenical response to military repression, many priests, nuns, pastors, numerous lay people and bishops of the Catholic and Protestant churches of Argentina worked to realize national unity and peace, establish solidarity with those whose fundamental rights had been negated, to promote education in human rights and denounce the violation of human rights. Priorities were quickly established, empowering the organizations of the relatives of victims of forced disappearance and of political prisoners, assisting ex-detainees and prisoners and returning exiles to find jobs and housing, including using their skills to join the staff of MEDH and its growing regional chapters across Argentina, working on behalf of the rights of children and adolescents, and later, developing a pastoral ministry among victims of HIV-Aids. Throughout, the WCC and national agencies related to the churches worldwide accompanied closely the work of MEDH, which became a key partner in the strengthening network of ecumenical organizations (and teams of men and women) within the region.

The APDH

In September 1975, a group of people organized a press conference to denounce the killing, disappearances and attacks of the right-wing AAA. The initiative led to the formation of the Permanent Assembly for Human Rights,[10] officially founded on 18 December 1975, which was a pluralistic organization incorporating people with different ideological, political, religious and social perspectives, yet all committed to confronting and denouncing the human rights violations taking place in Argentina under the military Junta: leaders of political parties, trade unionists and representatives of Catholic, Protestant and Jewish religious groups. It engaged in vast education campaigns designed to inform ordinary citizens of their rights under the Constitution and International Law and for the restoration of democratic rule. Its membership included, among many other persons, Jaime Schmirgeld, Eduardo Pimentel, Carlos Gattinoni, José Míguez Bonino, Susana Pérez Gallart, Alfredo Bravo, Simón Lázara, Raúl Alfonsín (later elected president of the Nation in 1983) and Graciela Fernandéz Meijide. Ms Meijide, a mother of one of the disappeared, and one of the permanent fighters for justice at the core of the APDH, rose quickly after 1983 to become one of the leaders of a centre-left coalition[11], and won a seat in the nation's senate in mid-1990.[12] We were privileged to have known and accompanied the work of the APDH for many years since its inception and founding in 1975. Along with other human rights organizations in Argentina which fulfilled public advocacy roles, such as the *Servicio Paz y Justicia* (founded in 1974 by Adolfo Pérez Esquivel) and the *Centro de Estudios Legales y Sociales* (CELS), founded later in 1980 by Emilio Mignone and Augusto Comte, the APDH was a keen and courageous observer and actor on the public stage, denouncing the abuse of states of emergency and judicial aberrations while calling for a rapid transition to democracy and for the implementation, by the State, of its obligations towards its citizens in the area of human rights. One of the many risky and effective achievements of the APDH consisted in secretly importing, in large camouflaged boxes, hundreds of copies of the damning report on the state of human rights in Argentina, prepared and published in 1980 by the Interamerican Commission of Human Rights of the Organization of American States. APDH continues today in its efforts to achieve justice in Argentina, to hold all those responsible for violations accountable, and to ensure their prosecution.

The horror

It is difficult, if not impossible, to imagine the systematic destruction of human life organized from the moment the military *Junta*[13] took office. It is here where the historic contribution to the collective memory, represented by the mammoth accomplishment of the Argentine National Commission on the Disappeared, CONADEP,[14] becomes the vehicle of what is impossible to imagine. In a significant move, President Raúl Alfonsín appointed the Commission, under the presidency of the writer Ernesto Sábato, to receive testimony from the many families whose relatives had been abducted by the army, police or security forces, and made to "disappear", but it also received much information from a variety of sources. Carlos Santiago Nino, one of President Alfonsín's human rights advisors who was a witness to CONADEPS's work, writes:[15]

CONADEP began its duties on 29 December 1983 by appointing Ernesto Sábato as president and designating five secretaries to handle specific tasks: Graciela Fernández Meijide became the secretary in charge of receiving denunciations. ... It inspected 340 clandestine detention centers and visited morgues and cemeteries in order to identify corpses ... and inspected registers of the police and of prisons. Members of the commission went to military garrisons, prisons, and mental hospitals that had been identified as places where some of those who had disappeared could be found; the results were always negative. ... With the cooperation of the Abuelas de la Plaza de Mayo, CONADEP helped create a data bank in the Durán Hospital that would help identify and return to their relatives children born to women in detention. Those children had been "adopted" during the military regime. In the course of the proceedings, CONADEP received testimony covering fifty-thousand file pages on seven thousand different cases. Certain testimony was extremely forceful and effective.

Its final Report stunned Argentinians when it was published in 1984 and became the principal instrument of persuasion for the body politic to press for the trials of the members of the Junta, which took place during a year later in 1985.

In order to understand the depths of suffering undergone by thousands of Argentine citizens, and the depravity of its perpetrators, one should plunge into the reading of the Report in full. Clearly, to reproduce even one chapter of it will not be possible here. Nonetheless, a brief quote from some of the words contained in the Prologue of the Commission's report, by its president, Ernest Sábato, will provide a short glimpse of the abyss it describes and of the significance of its findings. It will help us to understand its impact, while communicating to us the context and climate in which the human rights organizations carried on during those seven years of military rule:

> From the huge amount of documentation we have gathered, it can be seen that these human rights were violated at all levels by the Argentine state during the repression carried out by its armed forces. Nor were they violated in a haphazard fashion, but systematically, according to a similar pattern, with identical kidnappings and tortures taking place throughout the country. How can this be viewed as anything but a planned campaign of terror conceived by the military high command? ...
>
> The abductions were precisely organized operations, sometimes occurring at the victim's place of work, sometimes in the street in broad daylight. They involved the open deployment of military personnel, who were given a free hand by the local police stations. When a victim was sought out in his or her home at night, armed units would surround the block and force their way in, terrorizing parents and children, who were often gagged and forced to watch. They would seize the persons they had come for, beat them mercilessly, hood them, then drag them off to their cars or trucks, while the rest of the unit almost invariably ransacked the house or looted everything that could be carried. The victims were then taken to a chamber over whose doorway might well have been inscribed the words Dante read on the gates of Hell: "Abandon hope, all ye who enter here".
>
> All sectors fell into the net: trade union leaders fighting for better wages; youngsters in student unions; journalists who did not support the regime; psychologists and sociologists simply for belonging to suspicious professions; young pacifists, nuns and priests who had taken the teachings of Christ to shanty areas; the friends of these people, too, and the friends of friends, plus others whose names were given out of motives of personal vengeance, or by the kidnapped under torture. The vast majority of them were innocent... (...)
>
> From the moment of their abduction, the victims lost all rights. Deprived of all communication with the outside world, held in unknown places, subjected to barbaric tortures. Kept ignorant of their immediate or ultimate fate, they risked being either thrown into a river or the sea, weighed down with blocks of cement, or burned to ashes. They were not mere objects, however, and still possessed all the human attributes: they could feel pain, could remember a mother, child or spouse, could feel the infinite shame at being raped in public. They were people not only possessed of this sense of boundless anguish and fear, but also, and perhaps indeed because of feelings such as these, they were people who, in some corner of their soul, clung to an absurd notion of hope.

We have discovered close to 9,000 of these unfortunate people who were abandoned by the world. We have reason to believe that the true figure is much higher...

All we are asking for is truth and justice, in the same way that the churches of different denominations have done, in the understanding that there can be no true reconciliation until the guilty repent and we have justice based on truth.[16]

Mauricio

One the abductions which most pained and mobilized the ecumenical community, nationally and worldwide, was that in which the victim was Professor Mauricio Amilcar López, on 1 January 1977. He was, as noted above, a devoted member of the inner circle of ecumenical leaders in Mendoza[17] during the Chilean exodus. A professor of Philosophy and a member of the *Iglesia de los Hermanos Libres*, he was also a respected figure, a *Homo Oecumenicus*[18] of great stature and spiritual depth, whose contributions to social and theological thought in Latin America, to the WCC and to the ecumenical family have been widely recognized. He had served as the Latin America Secretary of the World Student Christian Federation and later became the Secretary of the Department on Church and Society of the WCC. In this position he was a key organizer of the 1966 World Conference on Church and Society held in Geneva and influenced greatly the creation of the ecumenical movement of the same name (ISAL, or *Iglesia y Sociedad en América Latina*) which was to have a preponderant influence on the new generation of emerging Christian leadership in the region. His whereabouts were never communicated to his family in Mendoza. However, it would seem that strong evidence pointed to the responsibility of the Fourth Brigade of the Air Force,[19] in the abduction and killing of Mauricio Lopez, with several other persons, at a clandestine centre named Las Lajas, near Mendoza.[20]

Abuelas de la Plaza de Mayo

One of the most courageous and effecive of such human rights groups are the Grandmothers of the Plaza de Mayo.[21] Among the many disappeared in Argentina were children, abducted along with their parents, as well as infants born to women who were pregnant when they were abducted by the security forces or death squads. In many instances the children and the infants were secretly given away for adoption to families ideologically favoured by the military junta. The *Associación Abuelas de la Plaza de Mayo* was created by grandmothers trying to trace their disappeared grandchildren, both those kidnapped with their parents and those believed to have been born in the prisons and detention centres. The intiative behind this was taken in 1977, by Maria Isabel Ch. de Mariani, who, searching for her own grand-daughter Clara Anahi Mariani,[22] met with several other grandmothers looking for their grandchildren. Under Sra Mariani's leadership over the years, the Association has grown in strength and public esteem, with the support of many persons in Argentine society and international friends. Today, it is estimated by the Abuelas that over seven–hundred children were taken from their parents or born in some of the 340 detention centres around the country during those years of the "dirty war". Some were brutally murdered, as was revealed when forensic teams discovered evidence of such atrocities in common graves.

The *Abuelas* developed a strategy for locating missing children which included investigating all adoptions granted by juvenile or federal courts since 1976, checking the civil register for unusual birth registrations, disseminating information about disappeared children through newspaper advertisements and posters, and making inquiries in various neighbourhoods. Eighty of these grandchildren have been located over the years. DNA tests were often made also, comparing the genetic marker of a paternal grandparent and maternal grandmother with that of a located child. The pioneering work of the Abuelas was a major reason why the new civilian government of Argentina established the National Genetic Data Bank to determine the blood groups and antigen of surviving relatives of the children, and to store blood samples for DNA identification. In this way, when and if other "children" are found, they will be able to check with the data bank to learn of their maternal ancestry, using the samples left behind by the grandmothers.[23] The campaign of the Grandmothers also led to the re-arrest, in 1998, of Argentina's first members of the Junta, General Jorge Videla and Admiral Emilio Massera, on charges of abducting children.

In February 1999 the Association of the Grandmothers of the Plaza de Mayo received the Methodist Peace Prize from the World Methodist Council for its work, awarded to its current president, Estela Barnes de Carlotto, for its "courage in their pursuit of the missing children and infants in the face of brutal repressions".[24] At a ceremony marking the fiftieth anniversary of the WCC, Geneviève Jacques, an Executive Secretary for international affairs, remarked that "beyond the return of their grandchildren … the purpose of the grandmothers' struggle is to demand that the whole truth be told and justice be done for the crimes of the past".[25]

The WCC has accompanied the work of the *Abuelas* since its inception. One of the most rewarding moments for visiting members of the ecumenical community at the *Abuelas* headquarters, has been that of enjoying a cup of tea and biscuits with these remarkable women, surrounded – when schools in Buenos Aires were on vacation – by some of those located girls and boys who formed a support group for their grandmothers and who joined them for their monthly meetings. The *Abuelas* continue their work today, undaunted.

Members of WCC's Central Committee met in Buenos Aires, 28 July-8 August, 1985. They will remember the evening, organized by the MEDH and the host Argentine member churches of the WCC, during which time the history of the struggle for human rights in Argentina was described and strongly evoked by numerous witnesses and spokespersons from the various human rights organizations in Argentina. A particularly searing testimony was that of Pablo Diaz, the sole survivor of a group of eight teenagers who had been kidnapped on 16 September 1976.[26] Their ages ranged from fourteen to eighteen years. They had been taken from their various homes to clandestine centres, tortured and killed because they had been demanding a reduced rate in public transportation for students. It was an emotional moment when, at a ceremony closing the evening, one of the located children, Paula Eva Hogares, then aged ten, and accompanied by Maria Isabel de Mariani, walked with several other children among the delegates lighting the candles of peace.

The Argentine Forensic Anthropology Team (EAAF) [27]

Another remarkable group of persons took shape in 1984, young forensic graduate students in Buenos Aires, who began carrying out serious, scientific exhumations of the remains of thousands of unidentified victims of the repression, who had been buried in anonymous graves or in free areas of local cemeteries throughout the country. Under the initial guidance of Dr. Clyde C. Snow, a foremost expert in forensic anthropology, this team exhumed and attempted to identify the remains of disappeared persons, collecting evidence for court cases involving human rights and – certainly as important – assisting the loved ones of these victims to recover the remains, to carry out the customary funeral rites and find closure. The MEDH provided the physical office space, in the mid-1980s, for the administrative work of the team.

At first the team worked in the investigation of bodies which were found along the Uruguayan coast during the Argentina dictatorship.

The bodies were thought to correspond to people who "disappeared", then were dumped into the Atlantic Ocean and the Argentine sea by security forces from Argentinian Air Force airplanes. The corpses were found by Uruguayan coast guards at the time and buried as unidentified persons in local cemeteries.[28]

These flights were later described in 1995 by Navy captain, Adolfo F. Scilingo, who told a well known investigative reporter in Argentina, Horacio Verbitsky,[29] that he had participated in flights conducted by the Argentine Navy in 1976 and 1977. Before the flights, the prisoners were injected with a sleep inducing drug, Pentonaval, and "when they became unconscious, they were stripped naked and dropped from the planes". Scilingo went on trial in January 2005, in a Spanish court, accused of the murder of political prisoners and facing charges of war crimes, genocide, torture and terrorism.

Since 1986 the EAAF has trained other groups in Latin America and the Caribbean, working alongside teams in Chile, Bolivia, Paraguay, Brazil, Venezuela, Peru, Colombia, El Salvador, Guatemala, Panama, Honduras and Haiti (as well as in the Philippines, Ethiopia, Romania, Croatia, Iraqi Kurdistan, French Polynesia, and South Africa) – in each case applying multi-disciplinary techniques and methods to exhume, establish the cause of death and identify the skeletal remains of victims of human rights violations in these countries. It has rendered an indispensable service to the families of victims across the continent and to the human rights community as a whole.

Stimulated to a great extent by the findings of the CONADEP ("Sábato") Report, the Supreme Court brought the top military chiefs responsible for the "dirty war", to trial on 22 April 1985. The hearings, open to the public and broadcast daily on national television, lasted until August. The prosecutor, Julio Strassera, summed up his conclusions by requesting severe punishment for all the members of the three juntas. The sentences handed down by the Federal Court sentenced life imprisonment for General Jorge Videla and Admiral Emilio Massera; seventeen years for Brigadier Orlando Agosti, eight for Admiral Armando Lambruschini and permanent disqualification from holding public office for all four. However, trials involving the great majority of second-level and lower levels of officers and military personnel were not able to be carried out because of a "full-stop" law enacted by Congress on 23 December 1986.

Just two weeks before it was finally enacted, the leaders of the Ecumenical Movement for Human Rights (MEDH) issued a strong public statement, reflecting the wide consensus among the population against this curtailment of the judicial process.

Keep far from a false charge, and do not slay the innocent and the righteous, for I will not acquit the wicked (Exodus 23:7)

The Ecumenical Movement for Human Rights declares its total rejection of the draft law on termination of criminal proceedings against the members of the Armed Forces, the Police, Security and Prison services. As Christians committed to the protection of life, we think it necessary to reflect with the people of which we are a part, on the contents of the above initiative and on its implications.

The Draft Law, by putting a *Punto Final* (Full Stop) to legal investigations into the situation of thousands of persons who have disappeared, to the trial and condemnation of those guilty of abduction, torture, murder and the kidnapping of children and theft of the victims' property, is in violation of ethical principles which should not be abandoned, and is in flagrant contravention of the constitutional principle which guarantees equality under the law.

If the law proposed by the National Executive is approved, those who committed atrocious crimes in secret after subverting constitutional order will be rewarded. Those who concealed evidence of this criminal action will be equally encouraged, as well as the complicit inaction of the military courts. The passivity of the federal courts which failed to live up to their responsibilities to press for an indictment of the crimes, will be prized. A mockery will be made of those who testified truthfully and courageously before the commissions of legislative investigation and to the National Commission on the Disappearance of Persons, set up at the time by the President of the Nation before the Federal Court of the national capital. The Court's mission was entrusted by us with constitutional powers to ensure the triumph of truth and justice, in spite of all the obstacles which were placed in its path.

In the name of human rights, we energetically call upon our legislators to refrain from sanctioning any rule which would cripple the essential actions of the courts, but rather to enact legislation to make its proceedings more efficient and correct. In this manner they will lend their valuable support to reconciliation among the populations of our nation, which we hope will strengthen democracy for the peaceful achievement of greater justice, liberty and a community spirit.

Immediately following the passing of this debilitating legislative action to curtail the trials, the courts acquitted fifteen admirals of the responsibility for crimes committed on the grounds of the Naval Mechanics School (ESMA). Years later, on 29 December 1990, President Carlos Menem signed another set of pardons, freeing those already convicted for human rights violations, including all who had been sentenced in 1985.[30]

So, why are Christians involved in human rights?

During the 1985 evening event on human rights at the meeting of the WCC's Central Committee mentioned above, José Míguez Bonino, one of the presidents of the APDH, spoke with great insight and passion of the fundamental bases of Christian involvement in the struggle for the defence of life:

> We are going to speak about human rights. What do those words suggest? A set of legal provisions? A problem for some regions, such as the Third World and the countries of the East, a problem that we have already solved? A weapon in international conflicts? A hobby for a particular interest group? Such superficial conflicts can only divert us from the basic issues...
>
> Individuals, groups and peoples, because of their experience of oppression, are crying out for the humanity that is being denied them. And that cry and that struggle enable them to discover human dignity and establish its underlying principles... That has happened in the past, is still happening today, and is happening ecumenically: from oppressive regimes, to hunger in Africa, passing through the suffering in Lebanon, marginalization and cultural destruction or genocide of indigenous peoples, and the oppression of women and their being reduced to mere objects.
>
> If we are speaking today of Argentina, that is not because the situation here is particularly important or exceptionally serious, but because our painful experience in this country and the struggle we are engaged in enable us to concentrate in one particular place on the pain, the struggles and the hopes of many human beings. For all suffering, all struggles, are the suffering and struggles of all, experienced by all. From this land, where you are today we want a call to go out to others to engage in reflection and commitment, we hope, just as we ourselves have responded to the call that others have addressed to us. Modestly and in hope, we simply share what we have experienced.
>
> What have we learned here in these years about the struggle for human rights? Everyone could, of course, identify different things. However, I do believe that we could all agree on at least three points...
>
> 1. We have learned that human rights form one single indissoluble whole: guarantees and rights for individuals, economic and political rights and the right of peoples to self-determination – they all depend on one another and define one another...
> 2. The struggle for human rights cannot be the task of a group of militants or of a particularly enlightened people. To be effective it must become a struggle by all the people...

3. We are learning – and this is essential in the difficult process of establishing and securing democracy – that three indispensable aspects are interrelated: the moral principles on which the life of a people rests; respect for life and the dignity of the person, solidarity, truth and justice; and a plan or vision of the nation that we want to see, i.e. a democracy with participation and social justice...

Again, each one of these aspects strengthens, involves and interpenetrates the other...

We Christians who have shared in this struggle have learned one further foremost and basic thing. For us it is not a matter of simple moral duty or humanitarian work (both of value in themselves). What was at stake was the authenticity of our faith, our witness to our claim to bear the name of Christian.

I believe in God, the Almighty, the Creator. And thus we accept with thanksgiving the gift of life, we affirm it and we commit ourselves to preserve, defend and enhance it.

I believe in Jesus Christ, our Lord, who was born, suffered, died and rose again, and is at the Father's right hand. And thus we believe in the dignity of all human beings, God's sons and daughters, our brothers and sisters by the redemption of the Crucified One, called to a new life, exalted with the Risen One and destined to eternal life.

I believe in the Holy Spirit. And thus we believe in hope, beyond all objective or subjective possibilities or impossibilities, because God's Spirit is let loose in the world until the end of time. And, where the spirit is – whatever may be the conditions or powers of oppression or death – there is freedom.

I believe in the Most Holy Trinity. And thus we affirm an eternal communion of love, not invented or created by ourselves, enfolding the whole of humankind and drawing us onward into that eternal communion of love, by sharing in which we reach our full humanity.

That is why we believe and struggle for human rights. And in that struggle we are giving witness to our faith.

NOTES

[1] According to an internal progress report of the WCC, dated June 1974, addressed to cooperating church-related agencies.
[2] Cf. the reference to its work in the previous chapter (Chile).
[3] Notably, by members of the so-called "Triple-A", the Anti-Communist Alliance of Argentina (AAA), a right-wing death squad under the control of a man called López Rega. This organization was responsible for the murders of over two hundred people, by September 1974, according to Buenos Aires professor Carlos Santiago Nino (*Radical Evil on Trial*, New Haven: Yale University Press, 1996, p. 52).
[4] Within their organizations named here, Oscar Bracelis, Pastor Alieda Verhoeven and Prof Mauricio López were key leaders in mobilizing support for the refugees.
[5] From the Introduction, by Ronald Dworkin, to *Nunca Más: the Report of the Argentine National Commission on the Disappeared* (New York: Farrar Straus Giroux, in association with Index on Censorship, 1986), p. xii.

[6] Argentine Anticommunist Alliance.

[7] The Ecumenical Movement for Human Rights.

[8] This evaluation was part of many contributions made during an important meeting, held in Santiago de Chile from 20-23 October 2003, entitled "Thirty Years of Ecumenical Commitment with Dignity and Human Rights". Representatives of the ecumenical and church-related human rights organizations in the Southern Cone of Latin America, Brazil and Peru, shared the rich legacy of these organizations active in the period from 1970 to the present, made a critical analysis of their work and of the record of the churches in the area of human rights defence, and laid out some challenges confronting them today. The author has drawn upon the conclusions and recommendations of the encounter in this narrative and is grateful to the organizers (FASIC and the WCC) for his having been invited to participate in the encounter.

[9] *Movimiento Ecuménico por los Derechos Humanos, Documento Base: Si Cristo con Nosotros Quien Contra Nosotros.* Argentina, 9 July 1976.

[10] *Asamblea Permanente por los Derechos Humanos.*

[11] FREPASO.

[12] Dafne Sabanes Plou, in *Latinamerica Press* (Lima), Sept. 18, 1997, p. 3.

[13] General Jorge Rafael Videla (Army), Admiral Emilio Eduardo Massera (Navy) and Brigadier Orlando Ramón Agosti (Air Force).

[14] *Comisión Nacional sobre la Desaparición de Personas* (National Commission on the Disappearance of Persons).

[15] Santiago Nino, op. cit., pp. 78-79.

[16] Nunca Más, op. cit., pp 2-5.

[17] Notably as a member of the team of the Fundación Ecuménica de Cuyo.

[18] Attributed to him by Julio de Santa Ana, in the preface to a two-volume collection of the written works by Maurício Lopez: *Los Cristianos y el Cambio Social en la Argentina: Panorama Histórico Social 1965-1975 (Tomo I)* and *Analisis de Documentos (Tomo II). Edited by Oscar Bracelis* (Mendoza: A.P.E. and P.E.C., 1989).

[19] Under the supervision and authority of Luciano Benjamín Menéndez, Commander of the *Tercer Cuerpo* of the Army for the entire district.

[20] As reported in the national daily newspaper *Clarín*, 2 June 2004, based on sworn testimony by Eduardo Luis Duhalde, then the Secretary for Human Rights of the Ministry of Justice, in a declaration before the Federal Court of Appeals.

[21] Abuelas de la Plaza de Mayo, created in 1977.

[22] Clara Anahí was born on 12 August 1976, and was abducted three months later, on 14 November while her mother Diana E. Teruggi and others there were murdered on the spot. Her father, Daniel Mariani was detained and assassinated eight months later. Clara Anahí is believed to be alive and well, but in spite of herculean efforts made by the Association and her grandmother for these past thirty years, she has not yet been located.

[23] See "Medical News and Perspective: Mitochondrial DNA Studies Help Identify Lost Victims of Human Rights Abuses", in *JAMA*, April 21, 1993 Vol. 269, No. 15.

[24] by Dr Joe Hale, WMC general secretary.

[25] Stephen Brown, "Argentina's famous grandmothers win Methodist Peace Prize", *ENI Bulletin*, Number 02 (17 February 1999), p. 13.

[26] *"La noche de los Lapices"* (the Night of the Pencils).

[27] Equipo Argentino de Antropologiá Forense (EAAF).

[28] "Argentine Forensic Anthropology Team, Biannual Report 1994-95".

[29] *El Vuelo*, op. cit.

[30] Nino, op. cit., p. 104.

6
The Condor's Nest
Paraguay

Paraguay has an area of 406,752 square kilometres and a population of 3,600,000. Like Bolivia, it is one of the two landlocked countries in South America. Population density is 8.5 persons per square kilometre. Authoritarianism has always been a feature in the country's history. When independence from Spain came in 1811 dictatorships of Rodríguez de Francia, C.A. López and F.S. López took the form of a despotism unparalleled in the rest of the continent. Paraguay endured two international wars, one from 1865 to 1870 during which time it lost half its population and large amounts of land in a vicious dispute with Brazil, Argentina and Uruguay over access to the sea. The second time from 1932 to 1935 with Bolivia. A number of civil wars – the latest being in 1947, racked the country. The dictatorship of General Alfredo Stroessner made authoritarianism secure with the hegemony of a tiny group in the socio-economic structure of Paraguay....

Thus begins an introduction to the report by an ecumenical delegation[1] to Paraguay in October 1988, which had been invited by the Comité de Iglesias para Ayudas de Emergencia (CIPAE)[2] and by the Misión de Amistad,[3] both ecumenical organizations based in Asunción. At the time, these church organizations were coming under pressure by the authorities for their work among marginalized sectors of Paraguayan society and for their pastoral and social assistance to political prisoners and their families

It was only a year before President Stroessner was deposed in a coup led by General Andrés Rodríguez and fled the country to receive asylum in Brazil. It was therefore a period, during 1988, when repression was particularly severe, targeting base organizations and intermediary groups committed to popular aspirations. The report of the delegation stressed that

A deep impression was made on the people's consciousness by the way General Alfredo Stroessner's dictatorship has been contriving for thirty-four years (since 1954) to present itself as the sole guarantor of peace in the country and imputing every kind of evil to any possibility of change in the political and social structure. ... Particularly at this time persecution is focussed on the base organizations. ... Their leaders and members are surrounded by a menacing atmosphere of strict surveillance, tapping of telephone calls, telex services and correspondence in general. ...

Indeed, this regime, although hidden behind a façade of controlled general elections, was the oldest in this part of the Southern Cone, and was notorious since the 1954 coup d'état engineered by General Stroessner, for its wide-scale arrests and the forced disappearance of political opponents and, often, their families, for long term detention without trial and the systematic use of torture.[4] As we shall see below, General Stroessner also participated in, fomented and hosted the infamous plan to eliminate political opposition in a secret operation called CONDOR, in the countries of the Southern Cone, along with military leaders Augusto Pinochet (Chile), Jorge Videla (Argentina), Hugo Banzer (Bolivia), João Figueredo (Brazil) and the civilian president of Uruguay, Juan Bordaberry.

CIPAE

It was because of the mass arrests, in 1976, of over three-hundred persons active in the Roman Catholic Church and other organizations that the first CIPAE team came into action, under the protection of the Roman Catholic Archbishop of Asunción, Ismael Rolón. Rapidly, two other churches became members of CIPAE, the Evangelical Church of the River Plate (with Pastors Hôner and Ihle representing it), and the Disciples of Christ (Pastor Luis de Pilar). Most of the prisoners mentioned above were taken to the prison of Embuscada, some 70 kilometres from Asunción, where the first social workers of CIPAE brought family members and food, and where they attempted to visit detainees maintained incommunicado, with humanitarian assistance. This is when the WCC first began its long relationship of visits, support and "accompaniment", through staff but as well in conjunction with representatives of member churches and human rights groups in neighbouring countries, especially Brazil and Argentina

CIPAE, presently led by Lic. Cristina Vila, has been in the forefront of the struggle for the defence of human rights in Paraguay since its inception. In a real sense, it was a follow-up to the heroic work of Doña "Coca" Lara Castro, who for years had almost single-handedly confronted the Stroessner regime with evidence of its persecution and torture of Paraguayan citizens, through her *Comissión Paraguaya de Derechos Humanos.*

At the beginning CIPAE visited political prisoners in local police stations or other prisons during the heavy period of repression in the late 1970s, providing direct assistance to them in the form of food, medicine and educational and recreational materials, as well as legal assistance. Its teams also visited common law prisoners, who were detained under harsh prison conditions and were often subject to torture. CIPAE conducted studies on the Paraguayan situation and promoted peasant organizations, providing leadership and technical training. Its distinguished record includes providing assistance to refugees and migrants, and it promoted greater sensitivity to social problems in Christian communities, stimulating them to greater commitment and knowledge of the problems affecting society. In the rural areas CIPAE defended the land rights of peasant families. It has always coordinated its work closely with other non-governmental organizations in Paraguay, and in particular with human rights.

Among those were the Banco Paraguayo de Datos (BPD), an organization specializing in gathering data on the critical situation affecting the population in rural and urban areas. Staffed by social scientists, it provided services to national institutions with data on the economic, social, labour and political situation in Paraguay, and received assistance from many church and other sources internationally, including the WCC. Like members of the staff of CIPAE, members of the BPD also suffered detention for short periods of time, such as in May 1983, when its offices were raided by the police and several of its personnel[5] taken into custody.[6]

The Christian Church (Disciples) had long been present in Paraguay, with the Colegio Internacional which trained many generations of Paraguayans. Former students of the Colegio founded the Misión de Amistad (Friendship Mission) on 17 October 1953, in cooperation with the United Christian Missionary Society, of the USA, as an ecumenical body for social advancement. It carried out many programmes among the urban, rural and indigenous populations in Paraguay, providing comprehensive services in the area of health, agricultural engineering and education, community organization, culture and art in the poor neighbourhoods of Asunción. Its strong promotional approach to indigenous issues and social organization put the Mision de Amistad on the front line of human rights concerns, and it was a valuable ally during the Stroessner years as other Paraguayans moved ahead in setting up human rights organizations

The Centro de Estudios Humanitarios (CEDHU),[7] founded in 1986, became a keen partner of the human rights community with its investigation into and dissemination of human rights standards among the population, conducting especially research on humanitarian issues. CEDHU sponsored seminars and workshops in the area of education, focussing particularly on women's and children's rights

The need for recording the history of repression in Paraguay became a deep concern for those early leaders and participants of CIPAE. Thus, with the direct involvement of the WCC, a team of persons, under the direction of the first coordinator of CIPAE, Fr. José M. Blanch, SJ, gathered documentation and testimonies to produce a book, in 1991, in the style of the *Nunca Más* series, entitled *El Precio de la Paz*.[8] It contains, in the 131 pages of its appendix, the full list of names, by sector and occupation, date and place of detention, of all the political prisoners during the period of Stroessner's dictatorship, 1954-1989. Combined with the riveting accounts by individual witnesses to the repressive acts by State agents, the record constitutes a genuine contribution to restoring the memory of this era. CIPAE has continued this service by publishing a series of current works on the nature and scale of human rights violations.[9]

Operation Condor and the "Archives of Terror"

The discovery, on 22 December 1992, of an enormous archival collection[10] of documents in Asunción, brought to a glaring light the complicity of six military regimes of neighbouring states in the southern region of the continent. State terrorism was revealed undisputedly, as were plans for the physical elimination of political opponents, the exchange of prisoners and data on detainees, among military intelligence units in Uruguay, Argentina, Chile, Paraguay, Brazil and Bolivia. The plan was established, according to some of the documents discovered in the archive, in Chile on 25 November 1975 at a military intelligence meeting. It was on General Pinochet's 60th birthday. After the meeting, military teams were sent into neighbouring or distant countries to search for and kill their political opponents. It was in this way that Orlando Letelier, the former minister of foreign affairs under Allende, was killed in Washington, DC on 21 September 1976, along with Ronni Karpen Moffitt. Four months earlier two well-known Uruguayan political leaders, Zelmar Michelini and Hector Gutiérrez were found shot dead near Buenos Aires.

> The Spanish judge Baltazar sent to his counterpart in Paraguay, José Waldir Servín a list of documents related to the operation cited above and which implicated the former dictator Jorge Rafael Videla in crimes against humanity. This documentation, presumably found in the Archives of Terror, constitute irrefutable evidence of atrocities committed during the military dictatorship. ... The former dictator Alfredo Stroessner took active part in "Operation Condor", which developed in the Southern Cone, according to the proofs that were handed over by Hebe de Bonafina, president of the Mothers of the Plaza de Mayo, in Buenos Aires, to Judge Baltazar Garzón. ... Stressner is now enjoying asylum in Brazil since the month of February 1989.[11]

The consequences of the conspiracy remain strong even today, not only for recovery of the memory of atrocities committed thirty years ago, but for those in civilian authority who must deal with the growing pressure by victims and their families to bring the perpetrators to justice.

NOTES

[1] Members were Dr. Heinz-Joachim Held, Rev. Oscar Bolioli, the Right Rev. David R.J. Evans, Rev. Karl Ernst Neisel, Dr. William J. Nottingham, Lic. Dafne Sabanes Plou, Rev. Rodolfo R. Reinich, Rev. David A. Vargas, Rev. Jaime N. Wright and the author
[2] The Committee of Churches for Emergency Help.
[3] Friendship Mission, historically related to the work of the Christian Church (Disciples of Christ).
[4] Amnesty International, July 1976.
[5] Among them, Enrique Goossen and Roberto Villalba.
[6] News of these detentions, widely disseminated, was responded to with strong representations made to the Paraguayan government in the days following 20 May 1983, sent by the WCC and churches in the USA, Great Britain, (West) Germany, France, Switzerland and the Netherlands. This is an example of how CIPAE often worked, reporting such incidents through secure means to the ecumenical community outside Paraguay, but making sure that it was not mentioned as the source of the alert. It was a strategy which the WCC respected and applied in its relationships with partners and churches in the international community.
[7] Centre for Humanitarian Studies, whose director was Dra. Esther Prieto.
[8] Published in Spanish: see Appendix III.
[9] For example, the excellent *La Dictadura de Stroessner y los Derechos Humanos*, by José Luis Simon G., in its Nunca Más series, Vol. I (Asunción: Comité de Iglesias, 1990).
[10] See details on accessibility to the archives, in Appendix IV.
[11] From "Situación de los Derechos Humanos en el Paraguay", CIPAE, 1999.

7

Copper
Bolivia

This large landlocked, high altitude[1] country has had its territory amputated by disastrous past wars with its neighbours – with Chile between 1879 and 1883 when it lost its access to the Pacific Ocean and during the Chaco Wars of 1928-30 and 1932-35 against Paraguay. Its relatively small population of 9 million is made up principally – 60% – by indigenous Quechua and Aymara indigenous people, who have provided the overwhelming proportion of exploited mine-workers in the productive silver, copper and tin mines of the nation during the last century and a half. The contours of Bolivian political history reflect a similar pattern of sharp temperature contrasts and stunning instability, characterized by centuries of conflict and repression, from the defeat by the Spanish[2] of the remarkably creative, organized and authoritarian Inca Empire,[3] through a series of repressed indigenous revolts against the European masters and, after its independence in 1825, recurrent internal strife and a succession of presidents. Domestic conflict revolved essentially around who was able to control the production of the mines high in the Andes, the fruitful yields[4] of large land holdings, and oil and natural gas interests.

The first government which genuinely took into account the needs of indigenous peasants and miners, instead of defending the interests of the traditional elite was that of Victor Paz Estenssoro, in the so-called April Revolution in 1952. The period is often referred to among Bolivians as a generative one, which saw the beginnings of agrarian reform, the introduction of universal suffrage and the nationalization of the tin mines, but it did not succeed in the long run. In 1964 the Army, under General Rene Barrientos Ortuño, carried out one of the multiple historic *coups d'etat*, by occupying the Siglo XX mining complex, when many union leaders were deported from the country.[5] After the accidental death of General Barrientos, hopes rose with the rule, starting in 1970, of an honest and progressive military officer, General Juan José Torres. He became a powerful ally of workers and peasant unions, favouring political dialogue and freedom of association. It was to be his downfall, both personally (assassinated in Buenos Aires, a target of Operation Condor), and politically with the rise in influence and then rule, by a coup on 21 August 1971, of the most sanguinary of military dictators, General Hugo Banzer Suarez. His government lasted seven long years and brought in one of two most repressive periods in recent Bolivian history.[6]

Assassinations, political killings, massacres, torture, detentions, house arrests and political exile characterized this regime and provided the context for a growing groundswell of non-violent resistance, not only from powerful mining and urban labour unions (even if prohibited), student movements and workers' wives organizations (as we shall see below), but also the strong voice of the Catholic Church.

In 1974, the Roman Catholic Church spoke out defending the pastoral and prophetic work of priests accompanying workers and peasants, whose published document, *Evangélio y Violencia,* which denounced, among other crimes, "attacks on freedom of expression, ... threats and violence against magazines and radio stations attempting to exercise that freedom; detention and deportation of journalists; public defamation against which it is impossible to defend oneself, and which is never retracted by the Ministry of the Interior." Monseñor Jorge Manrique, Archbishop of La Paz, increasingly criticized the repressive actions of Banzer's regime.

Members of the religious orders, priests and lay people were being persecuted as never before, often detained, and others exiled. A discreet programme of material assistance to political prisoners was set up in 1976, run for the most part by priests and nuns of foreign religious orders – in particular those of Spanish origin. We recall with admiration how cash from ecumenical sources, and the meticulous record of accounts found their secure and undisturbed place in the multiple folds of religious habits and the well-worn satchels of Oblate *savoir faire.*[8]

Simultaneously the Evangelical Methodist Church, from its headquarters in the capital, initiated solid projects of solidarity throughout the country, counting on the vast network of indigenous pastors and lay persons making up its ranks. Consequently this member church of the WCC was to suffer harassment and grave pressure during the Banzer and Meza governments, among which was the detention and imprisonment of its Bishop Mortimer Arias.

Permanent Assembly of Human Rights in Bolivia

It was also during Banzer's regime, in the thick of arrests in 1976, that the ecumenical organization, Asamblea Permanente de los Derechos Humanos de Bolívia (APDHB), came into being, with the clear objectives to 1) work for the observance of human rights in Bolivia, as stipulated in the Bolivian Constitution, the Universal Declaration of Human Rights and the International Covenants, 2) to monitor and denounce human rights abuses and 3) to promote human rights education among the different social sectors. The Asamblea thrived under the courageous presidency of Jesuit Father Julio Tumiri and a strong representation of social and civil organizations and church leaders, including those of the Lutheran and Evangelical Methodist Churches.

Based on precise information it received from many sources, it published widely-read reports both nationally and internationally on such abuses as enforced disappearances, torture and extra-judicial executions. The APDHB also provided legal aid to victims and their families, particularly in the presentation of writs of Habeas Corpus for detained or disappeared persons. Father Tumiri was detained and almost lost his life in a raid upon the headquarters of the Central Obrera Boliviana (COB) which occurred on 17 July 1980, where an emergency meeting of the leaders of a wide coalition of political parties, labour unions and human rights groups (CONADE) was being held on the very day that Luis García Meza launched his coup.

The WCC officers, meeting in Geneva soon after, sent one of the strongest messages it had ever before drafted, informing the member churches of the Council, members of its Central Committee and national and regional councils, of the "grave and massive violations of fundamental human rights in the country", deploring the loss of life resulting from the coup d'état and calling on the world-wide community to "uphold the churches of Bolivia as they undertake their pastoral and prophetic ministries", including generous support for their humanitarian programmes, and appealing to the churches to "urge their governments, intergovernmental organizations and other bodies to press for their support to the democratically-elected government of National Unity" which had been overthrown, and to "facilitate the re-establishment of democratic and political institutions in Bolivia".[9]

They were up against hardened criminals. The author distinctly recalls, in the late 1970s, being accompanied by the active pastor of the Lutheran German-speaking congregation, Pastor Gerhard Dümchen, to the edge of the parking lot of the international airport of La Paz, and being let out of the car there. "Unfortunately I cannot be seen with you inside because", warned my host, "you would be immediately searched and interrogated by the Banzer Army Intelligence Police (SEI) observing departing passengers on this Lufthansa flight". The reason being, as I rapidly discovered, that the experienced officer behind the smoked glass in the departure lounge was none other than Klaus "Altmann", later identified as Klaus Barbie, of Second World War notoriety as a ruthless Gestapo persecutor of Jews in the Lyon region in France.[10] It was under the Bolivian programme of extermination of political and civil opposition, enhanced with guidance from such infamous "human resources", that Jesuit priest Luis Espinal Camps, the director of the weekly *Aquí*, and a beloved film critic, was assassinated in 1981 by the death squad run by a personal friend of Klaus Barbie, Luis Arce Gómez, the right-hand man of General García Meza. Under the left-of-centre government of Hernán Siles Suazo, following the demise of Meza's government, Barbie was eventually expelled from Bolivia in February 1983 to face trial in France for crimes against humanity.

A seasoned group of women and men was already keenly aware of such activity. **The Association of Relatives of the Detained-Disappeared and Martyrs for National Liberation (ASOFAMD)** had been founded in 1970, so as to collectively confront repression. It was made up of the relatives of the disappeared or assassinated persons across the country and was independent of any political or religious affiliation. Its main aim, as is that of the region-wide network of the Associations of Relatives of Victims of Enforced Disappearance – FEDEFAM – is to obtain justice by trying and punishing those responsible for repressive acts, to develop public awareness of the significance of enforced disappearance and to reinforce democracy by dismantling the repressive institutions inherited from dictatorial periods. In this, it was a major supportive group which later successfully brought to trial Luis García Meza and his collaborators (see below). Its leader for many years, Loyola Guzmán, was also elected president of FEDEFAM, who, with its General Secretary, Patricio Rice, and accompanied by other non-governmental organizations, successfully nurtured and guided through the long administrative corridors and political maze of the United Nations, the above-mentioned draft convention on enforced disappearance which has recently been adopted (September 2005).

The hunger strike of 1978

Perhaps the most dramatic and unusual action which mobilized public and popular opinion in Bolivia, was the hunger strike initiated by four women and fourteen children – wives and children of mine workers banned from their jobs for union activity. It was in mid-January 1978. "In the Bolivian context what the women were demanding went beyond reason. They asked for an immediate, unrestricted amnesty for political exiles and refugees, restoration of jobs for workers fired for organizing, reinstatement of labour unions and removal of the army from the mines. But less than a month after they announced their goals, the movement they launched had forced the military dictatorship of General Hugo Banzer to grant the substance of all their demands".[11] According to the miners' families, in a report widely disseminated three months earlier – October 1977 – a member of a human rights association at the Siglo XX tin mine was arrested, beaten and tortured. Others were given the same treatment.

"The life of Bolivian tin miners and their families is a desperate affair. Though tin prices were then at their highest level in years, they received wages the equivalent of US$1.50 per day" and if a miner lost his job, his family had to move out of company housing, had no access to school for the children and were excluded from buying food at the company store.[12] Fifty miners' wives decided they had had enough, and designated four among them (Nellie Panigua, 45 years of age; Angelica Florés, 31; Aurora Lora, 25; and Luzmila Pimentel, 24) to go to La Paz to start the hunger strike. There they were joined by Domitila Chungara, 40, who used her skills as a spokesperson. At first it did not go well, as they were unable to generate support from groups either traumatized by the Banzer repression or wary of such a radical, albeit non-violent, approach. Soon, however, trade unions, churches (it started during the Christmas holiday) and ordinary people came forward, from scores to hundreds. Universities announced solidarity with them, other cities hosted hunger strikes. Most of the media reported it with sympathy. The government hardened its position, calling the strike subversive and sending the police to raid the offices of the left-of-centre *Presencia*.

The Roman Catholic Church then came in with strength, its prelates taking positions for justice. Nationwide demonstrations and mass opposition to the government from all sectors of society broke the government's resolve. President Banzer announced unrestricted amnesty on 18 January for all political exiles and prisoners, for new workers' rights and freedoms. It was a decisive victory of moral stamina and courage over a repressive regime totally unprepared for confronting the will of a united people.

The freedoms restored in Bolivia were short-lived. The 17 July 1980 coup brought General García Meza to power. He ruled for only thirteen months, but gross human rights violations were committed during his regime. The Socialist parliamentary representative, Marcelo Quiroga Santa Cruz was murdered – at the same meeting at the COB headquarters where the president of the APDHB, Fr. Tumiri, was arrested. Trade union leaders Gualberto Vega and Carlos Flores were also assassinated.

Committee to Bring Luis García Meza to Justice[13]
In early 1984, a trial against García Meza's dictatorship, called "Juicio de Responsabilidades" (Trial of Those Responsible) was initiated, under the leadership of Ivan Paz Claros, who was its General Secretary as well as that of the APDHB. In 1986 the Committee to Bring Luis García Meza to Justice was created to use all the channels possible to press for a just verdict in the "Juicio de Responsabilidades". This effort, which benefited, exceptionally, from the financial support of the WCC, ended with a successful outcome, with a sentence pronounced by the Supreme Court of Justice, in Sucre, in April 1993. Luis García Meza and the greater part of the accused were sentenced to thirty years in prison, with no possibility of pardon. Meza is serving his sentence in the prison of San Pedro de Chonchocoro. Significantly, this trial produced the one single successful sentence against a military figure accused of grave violations of human rights, who is serving out his sentence in jail, among all of his counterparts in Latin America.

NOTES

[1] From the tropical jungle to the north and the eastern lowlands to the cold Andean highlands above 3,500 metres.
[2] in 1538.
[3] They had developed an extremely efficient agricultural and irrigation system as well as sophisticated methods to refine gold and silver.
[4] Mainly wheat, maize, cotton and sugar.

[5] It was a violent period, with 520 persons who died murdered or who died for political reasons from 1964 to April 1969. 1173 persons were detained by the secret agency.

[6] The other being the short and brutal, drug-driven regime under General Luis García Meza, from 1980 to June of 1981.For a full narrative and analysis of Bolivian military repression and political history, see the excellent book by Lic. Federico Aguiló, *"Nunca Más" Para Bolivia* (Cochabamba: Asamblea Permanente de Derechos Humanos – APDHB & el Instituto de Estudios Sociales y Económicos de la Universidad Mayor de San Simón, de Cochabamba -IESE-UMSS, 1993).

[7] Aguiló, op. cit., p. 165.

[8] The author received generous hospitality at the Oblate priests' residence in a popular neighbourhood, during his multiple visits to La Paz. He is most grateful, especially to Fr. Gregorio Iriarte, as much for the fraternal conviviality and spiritual enrichment enjoyed in their company, as for the valuable orientation in Bolivian realities at the time.

[9] Letter dated 27 August 1980, and signed by The Most Rev. Edward W. Scott, Archbishop and Primate of the Anglican Church of Canada; Ms Jean Skuse, General Secretary of the Australian Council of Churches; His Holiness Karekin II, Catholicos Coadjutor, Armenian Catholicosate of Cilicia, and the Rev. Dr. Philip A. Potter, General Secretary of the WCC.

[10] Barbie had obtained Bolivian citizenship in 1957 after fleeing Europe and had quietly managed a lumber mill in northern Bolivia since 1951 under his assumed name. Being esteemed by General Banzer, also of German origins (along with Alfredo Stroessner of Paraguay with whom both maintained personal ties), he was hired to head the SEI, along with Jacques Edouard Lecrere (sic) of the former OAS, the right-wing clandestine organization which attempted to violently torpedo the Evian accords ending the French/Algerian civil war in 1962, and four other ex-Nazis from Germany and Austria who were transferred from Peron's Argentina to serve in Banzer's Ministry of the Interior after carrying out a number of political killings in Santa Cruz.

[11] From an article written by Wilson T. Boots, then pastor of Broadway Temple United Methodist Church in New York City. (*Christianity and Crisis*, 1 May 1979), p. 101. He went at that time to Bolivia as member of a joint WCC-NCCCUSA delegation of observers, along with Sister Jo Marie Griesgraeber, C.PP.S., deputy director of the Washington Office on Latin America (WOLA) and the Rev. Alan McCoy, O.F.M., representing the (US) National Conference of Catholic Bishops.

[12] Wilson, op. cit., p. 102.

[13] Comité Impulsor del Juicio de Responsabilidades contra Luis García Meza.

8
The Elegy
Peru

The lament of Zacarias Cconoce Huayhua, on finding his wife's body in a common grave, rung in the ears of the delegation from Lima, made up of international visitors[1] and of representatives of the national human rights community, visiting Ayacucho in October 1990. The grim discovery starkly illustrated the dilemma facing human rights advocates in Peru: how to distinguish the State-perpetrated violent actions from those of the Maoist Shining Path group? Members of the delegation were immediately confronted with the immense suffering and social breakdown of its population after ten years of insurgent and military terror.

> During the three days and nights spent in Huamanga, the provincial capital, substantial meetings were held with the representatives of social organizations, judicial institutions, church bodies, university faculty, the civilian authorities and the Political-Military Command. What emerged was a somber panorama of brutal murder, detention, torture, disappearance and abuse on a scale and to a degree barely tolerable among the majority indigenous population.[2]

We met with relatives of persons who had been rounded up in their high Andean villages – during the day if the Army surrounded them, in the middle of the night if they were elements of the *Sendero* insurgency. Inevitably, accounts of massacres – barely credible for their brutality – of campesinos and members of their families, regardless of gender or age tumbled from the words of Quechua women there to testify: straight-backed, focused, faces taut with restrained dignity.

Peru, a country with a dynamic population of twenty-eight million citizens, has, as in Bolivia, a majority population of indigenous people of Aymara and Quechua origins, who live for the most part in poverty, being excluded from the prosperity enjoyed by Peruvians of Spanish descent. Its recent history has shifted between periods of democratic rule and military dictatorship. Its social crises were particular evident during the 1980s, when the Shining Path rebels started actions to radicalize economic measures intending, theoretically, to benefit the majorities. Already, during the 1980s and by 1990, 20,000 lives had been lost in the struggle for the allegiance, or the repression, of the indigenous population, either perpetrated by the insurgents or by the Army and civil defence patrols linked to it. It reached the figure, according to some local sources, of 70,000 killed by the end of the decade of the 1990s.

In 1989, the economy was in dire shape, in spite of efforts made by previous civilian governments to redress a situation where inflation was close to 3000 per cent annually and a minimum wage of less than US$50 per month.[3] It may explain the reason why Peru is a leading producer of coca leaves, whose sale provides a much higher income for peasants.

The election of Alberto Fujimori, in 1990, created some hope for more stable economic conditions and for achieving a modicum of social peace. It prompted the Peruvian National Human Rights Coordinating Committee to invite the widely representative ecumenical delegation to visit Peru so as to enter into dialogue with the new government about the situation of human rights in the country, to give support to the churches, institutions and persons involved in the promotion and defence of human rights in Peru, and to promote international solidarity with all those who suffer the consequences of violence being experienced in the nation.

The National Coordinating Committee (CNDDHH) is a coordinating body for those organizations and groups active in Peru in the defence and promotion of human rights. It was created in 1985 and counted among its leading organizations the Pro-Human Rights Association (CEAPAZ), the Institute of Legal Defence, the Andean Commission of Jurists, the Commission for Human Rights (COMISEDH), the Association for Human Rights (APRODEH) and the Bishops' Commission for Social Action (CEAS). For its "commitment and dedication to human rights in the face of great adversity and threat to personal safety" the CNDDHH received the 1990 Letelier-Moffitt Human Rights Award in Washington, DC, USA, which was given to its Director, Pilar Coll, along with Miguel Talavera, Hortensia Muñoz, José Burneo, Pablo Rojas and Ernesto Alayza. In the 1990s it counted thirty organizations as members.

It was faced with a mammoth task in that year and the years following, with the Fujimori government. There were constant reports of persons forcibly recruited into the *rondas* of civilian patrols and of
astonishing cases of cholera epidemics, of malaria, tuberculosis and
other evidence of poverty and socio-economic crises. Political violence increased during the Fujimori era. Both government security
forces and the Shining Path operated with impunity and with disregard
for human life.

According to the Special Commission on Violence and Pacification of the
Peruvian Senate, chaired by Senator Enrique Bernales, an estimated 21,838
people have been killed in political violence since 1980 (of which 4,075 during the first fifteen months of Fujimori's government) More than sixty percent
of the victims of political violence have been peasants. .... . During 1991 there
has been a disturbing increase in attacks by new paramilitary groups: the Anti-
Terrorist Liberation Command and the Anti-Terrorist Alliance of Peru, taking
on the characteristics of death squads.[4]

The 1989 killing of six members of the Presbyterian churches in
the Altiplano, by Shining Path insurgents illustrated the suffering felt
by many Protestant communities severely victimized by political violence. This was brought forcefully to the attention of the ecumenical
community by the leadership of the Consejo Nacional Evangélico del
Perú (CONEP), a body of conservative Protestant evangelical
churches which had not seen fit to relate to the WCC in previous years.
However, given that, according to CONEP, some four hundred church
members had been assassinated as well as ten to twelve of their pastors
– crimes perpetrated by both sides of the conflict – various opportunities arose in 1989 and the early 1990s for the WCC to help channel
support to CONEP to minister to the needs of its congregations as they
faced grave violations of human rights.

Representatives of the Peruvian human rights organizations were
included annually, as were other representatives of churches and
related human rights organizations, in the ecumenical delegations
organized by the WCC and its Commission of the Churches on International Affairs (CCIA). Persons like José Burneo, (then) representing
CEAPAZ, contributed greatly to the understanding of the critical situation in Peru, by members of the Working Group on Forced Disappearances of the UN Commission on Human Rights.

In 2003, a Truth and Reconciliation Commission published its
findings in a far-reaching nine-volume report which substantiates the
evidence of crimes committed during the past twenty years in Peru

(the majority by Shining Path, but almost 30 per cent by the state agencies and the Army). Having carefully taken testimony from 17,000 witnesses, members of this commission confirmed the number of persons killed (69,000) during the two decades, and estimates the number of victims of forced disappearance at 1,800 to 2,000 persons. Recommendations for financial restitution to the victims are also strongly made, as they were also by the "Rettig" Truth Commission in Chile.

Despite the apparent destruction and neutralizing of the Shining Path insurgency and of more classic guerrilla groups such as the Tupac Amaru movement, violence continues in Peru, albeit to a much lesser degree than in the past.

NOTES

[1] Members of the delegation were: Ms Iona Victoria Campagnolo, former president of the Liberal Party of Canada and former Minister of Government, Canada; The Rev. Ryuichi Doi, Pastor of the United Church of Christ in Japan, and member of the National Diet (Lower House) of Japan; Monseigneur André Fauchet, Roman Catholic Bishop of Troye, France, former president of the Justice and Peace Commission of the French Episcopal Conference; the Rev. Gilberto Flores, Pastor of the Mennonite Church in Guatemala and representative of the Latin American Council of Churches (CLAI); the Very Rev. Sang Chul Lee, former Moderator of the United Church of Canada, former member of the Executive Committee of the General Council of the UCC; Mr. Thomas Loeb, Expert on social and economic development with the German Evangelical Church (EKD); Dr. José Antonio Martin Pallín, Magistrate of the Supreme Court of Spain, former president of the Pro-Human Rights Association of Spain; the Rev. Dr. Newton Thurber, former Associate General Secretary for Overseas Ministries of the National Council of the Churches of Christ in the USA; the Rev. Rolando Villena, Pastor and former Bishop of the Evangelical Methodist Church in Bolivia; and accompanying the delegation: the Rev. Charles R. Harper, Secretary of the Human Rights Resources Office for Latin America (HRROLA), WCC; Mr. William Fairbairn, Executive Director of the Interchurch Committee for Human Rights in Latin America, Canada; Ms Coletta Ann Youngers, Associate of the Washington Office for Latin America, Washington, DC, USA and Ms Muriel Juillard, Assistant of the HRROLA, WCC.
[2] from "Peru and Human Rights: Report of an International Ecumenical Delegation to Peru – 14–24 October 1990", p. 18.
[3] "Summary Report on the Human Rights Situation in Peru during 1989", by the National Coordination of Human Rights/Centre of Study and Action for Peace (CEAPAZ), published in cooperation with the WCC, p. 1.
[4] "Peru: One Year Later: Report of an International Ecumenical Delegation to Peru – 30 September –7 October 1991", p.7. This smaller delegation, made up of two members of the 1990 delegation (William Fairbairn and Rolando Villena,) and the Rev. Claude Dubois, representing the Canadian Religious Conference as well as Ms Stephanie Larson, representing the NCCCUSA, discovered a sharp escalation of violence, as can be seen, reported to them by the Peruvian human rights organizations.

9
What Lessons Have We Learned?

An assessment of the work of the Latin American churches, and that of the WCC in this area of concern suggests a certain number of lessons which we have learned. Reflection is a constant companion of action and of what one could call the spirituality of struggle – reaffirmed and nourished by a new sense of mission in many of the Latin American Christian communities.

1. Affirm the universality of rights. The efforts made to combat the use of torture are closely linked to the legitimate right of people to be free from economic and social injustice, which destroys life in many ways. One must identify the profound causes of this injustice, and attack it. Those who have fought for the respect of the civil and political rights of persons have learned – as does each generation in a critical period – that the combat against torture and for life cannot be seen in isolation from an affirmation of the basic rights of all, especially of the poor. The search for a sustainable, just society means that unjust economic and political structures must change. Consensus was reached among the churches regarding the content of human rights. Prolonged detention or torture are grave violations and must be seen as an encroachment on many inter-related rights, and an attempt by the State to weaken the struggle for all human rights.

2. Follow the lead of local actors in determining strategy. The nature of the struggle for human rights – for example, how to combat torture or work for a restoration of democracy – must be determined essentially by the national actors in this struggle. The most important work on human rights is carried out within the societies where its violations occur. Solidarity coming from outside is extremely important but it never replaces the mobilization of people within a country to combat injustices, defend the prisoner or work for freedom of expression. This is a challenge of major importance to the churches. It follows that we have found that enabling and equipping the local churches and groups takes priority over outside intervention. Faced with situations of violations of human rights, it is essential to strengthen and reinforce the actions which the churches and human rights groups pursue *in loco*. The oral and written interventions which were addressed by the WCC at the United Nations, for example, have been useful, but are complementary to what is accomplished nationally to garner forces for change. Effective strategies which are elaborated in a given society rest, as confirmed by the WCC Central Committee in 1979 "on the realization that those who live in any given location are best qualified to interpret and analyse their own experience".

3. Remember that realities motivate people. We have learned that one of the most important ingredients within the awareness-building process is that moment when people, such as those in parishes and congregations, were directly affected by repressive measures and when an opportunity was taken (or given) to reflect upon their experience with others, leading often to expressing the fruit of their reflection in published public statements and protests. Similarly, when we look at the many laws, declarations, bills and international covenants on human rights which have been developed over the years, they sound, as José Zalaquett has reminded us, "so principled and majestic that they are often taken as just a product of a happy blend of statesmanship and scholarship". Nothing is further from the truth. We have learned that these documents saw the light of day, in their time, because of the deep, painful and costly struggles of peoples and nations demanding recognition of their rights.

4. Recognize the importance of direct participation. We have learned that it is this concrete experience of the churches and individual Christians faced with the harsh violations of human rights which galvanized them to come to grips with what was happening around them and within their own membership. The experience roused them into creating new ministries of assistance to victims, of pastoral presence, of protection of people, of prophetic witness and towards an insistent call for justice. Military rule brought new awareness to congregations and parishes. They started from very small acts: assisting a mother and her children when a father was detained, giving shelter to a beaten student, finding transport for a labour union leader seeking escape into a neighbouring country, going to visit a prisoner under duress.

5. Pay close attention to non-traditional means in the struggle for human rights. Groups which were among the most creative in facing human rights violations were those which used unorthodox and non-academic means. There are many examples of this in the Latin American experience. One dramatic example was the hunger strike undertaken in early 1978 by four Bolivian miners' wives and their fourteen children, in the capital, La Paz. In a matter of days it shook and mobilized previously skeptical labour unions, the official church hierarchy, political parties and the establishment press. These women, modest but determined, received immediate support from base community human rights groups and it soon grew from strength to strength like a ground swell. The action finally led to a national show-down with the military regime, which allowed the return of exiles to the country and to the holding of the first democratic elections in nine years. What is notable here is that the action of these women was at first ignored, but then recognized, under popular pressure, as being genuine and effective by church leaders – who then responded with firm institutional support. The long years of military rule forged and disciplined mobilization among people, especially among those traditionally marginalized from economic and political arenas of power. These years also made people keenly aware of the numerical strength of majorities! These initiatives which use non-traditional means to mobilize support in favour of human rights are important and merit the support of the international community.

6. Work across social classes, professional sectors and geographic frontiers. If we wish to promote human rights in a given country most effectively, it is essential that all those involved understand mutually the specific *raison d'être*, strategy and action of each group and coordinate action accordingly. The exchanges of information and solidarity of all those who work for human rights, regardless of ideological or political differences and across borders between countries, have proved to be extremely valuable. The WCC learned to draw upon experiences, such as those of CLAMOR in Brazil, as it cooperated with groups representing families of disappeared persons in Uruguay, Argentina, Chile and Paraguay. In an inter-regional exchange coordinated with the Latin American Council of Churches and the Christian Conference of Asia, the WCC went further to enable ecumenical "militants" from six countries to visit each other's churches and to share vital experiences in the area of human rights.

7. "Learn from the biblical and theological reflection which has emerged from the churches' commitment to the cause of human rights. Their human rights work has engendered thoughtful insights and confessional positions. In Latin America, the contribution of theological "reflectors" has been been extremely helpful in articulating the roots of Christian commitment to human rights. For example, the late José Míguez Bonino, former dean of studies at Union Theological Seminary in Buenos Aires, Argentina, articulated eloquently the "confession of faith" of those Christians and churches engaged in the human rights struggle, at the Buenos Aires meeting of WCC's Central Committee in 1985:

"For Christians to be involved in the struggle, what is at stake is the very authority of our faith. Because we have faith we struggle for human rights and through our struggle we witness to our faith."

8. Work for unity in the struggle for change. The experience of many churches in Latin America has been that, to achieve basic change in a society or a regime, the churches had to unite with all the human rights organizations and social forces together in their struggle. The Argentinian experience is eloquent in this regard. In the early 1980s a dispirited and discredited military regime lost face and ground in the face of a vigorous national popular mobilization effort. That effort saw the Protestant evangelical churches and the human rights bodies make a significant contribution to a return to the rule of law and the election of a genuine (if fragile) democratic civilian government. It is an example of the unity required to strengthen what has become known as the "civil society" which emerged from the long fight against arbitrary rule: that is, a public opinion marked by a broad anti-military consensus, a political pluralism going beyond traditional bi-partisan control of government and a new generation of moderate, pragmatic, young democratic leaders intent on serving the needs of the people.

9. Be ready to confront division. We have seen that the struggle for human rights divides. It has been particularly divisive in situations where churches became the defenders of the *status quo*. In the words of the Latin American/Asian delegation report (1987), "whenever the Church becomes the defender of the status quo, it runs the risk of legitimising or acquiescing to repression which aims to preserve the status quo". Too often, Christians involved in the struggle for human rights have had to pay a high personal price for their solidarity. They have become isolated and little understood in their own church constituencies. The experience of fellowship in struggle uniting these faithful servants, which sprung up during these years of repression across the internal divisions of the churches and across denominational lines, bears within it the signs of resistance and hope.

10. Invest in and draw upon the credibility of the churches. In the international area of action, the WCC learned to build upon the undeniable credibility of the churches when they assumed major roles of protection, exercised prophetic witness and took significant leadership roles in Latin American countries. Thus, for example, the WCC was able to count upon the meticulous, substantiated information on the human rights situation which the church-related human rights organizations provided from various countries, so as to channel reliable data and information to churches worldwide, governments and agencies of the United Nations, so as to build effective international solidarity.

11. Never underestimate the value of ecumenical delegations and pastoral visits. We learned that we had to exercise great care to ensure that ecumenical delegations visiting these countries represented not only the wide scope of the ecumenical family but also include persons with expertise and whose experience demonstrated particular sensitivity to the issues which they would encounter – not to mention to the political stakes which were involved. These delegation visits took on increasing importance for the churches and for the WCC, moving beyond mere fact-finding missions, to become vehicles of serious dialogue, pastoral concern, sharing and mutual exchange. Ecumenical evaluations during and since those years have placed great importance on this form of action by the churches, as testified to within the seven countries discussed in this brief narrative.

12. Build upon existing relationships of trust. In the 1970s, as the WCC was called upon to respond to urgent calls from churches and ecumenical leaders during critical periods of repression, it intervened directly in a great number of situations to protect and provide rapid assistance to persons, in a variety of ways. So as to gain greater credible information and assessment of what was occurring, we rapidly drew upon existing historic relationships of trust which had been established and reflected through other programmatic commitments of the WCC in Latin America. For example, we received information and advice not only from regional individual members of the Commission of the Churches on International Affairs (CCIA – a "natural" environment of cooperation), but also from those persons related to historic inter-church aid projects with the Commission on Inter-Church Aid, Refugee and World Service, from those engaged with the Programme to Combat Racism, from those involved in development initiatives, with the Commission on the Churches Participation in Development, from the vast mission and evangelism representation in the Commission on World Mission and Evangelism – particularly from those involved in the activities of Urban and Rural Mission – from members of the Latin American Commission on Church and Society, from leaders of the Student Christian Movement and Youth movements, from health personnel linked to the Christian Medical Commission, from those engaged in theological and lay Christian education... (one could go on). The history of the way many of these persons and groups, often under severe pressure and attack themselves under military rule, came together in fresh ways under pressure, is impressive. It soon became a working principle, therefore, that if the international ecumenical family was to be effective in meeting human rights demands in the region, we had to work closely with this natural constituency of WCC partners. The principle was based on the conviction, justified time and time again, that the essential knowledge of the region's realities lay within its midst and that the levels of trust already there in the ecumenical community guaranteed its integrity.

13. Create specific networks of advice and coordination. A small group of ten to fifteen persons across Latin America – men and women heavily involved in their own situations – met regularly between 1975 and 1990, albeit informally, to analyse and to propose priorities for ecumenical action in human rights, and specifically to advise the office in the WCC which was responsible for coordinating its human rights work in the region. Alongside the official structures within the governing bodies and advisory task forces of the WCC, this parallel network provided the grist, immediacy and style for work. The network kept close communication with those key individuals in WCC's member churches in Latin America, as well as, after its formation, those of the human rights secretariat of the Latin American Council of Churches. The give and take, the sharing of essential trends, the mutual support and the sheer joy of fellowship which bound together those who participated – each coming out of tense and often dramatic situations requiring great stamina – proved to be invaluable.

14. Combine complementary methods of action. The WCC has learned that the most effective ecumenical international support for human rights has a multi-dimensional character. Great care was invested into combining various types of action: pastoral accompaniment, political analysis, advocacy and the development of funding mechanisms. International solidarity does not suppose only one form of action, or one particular approach, but rather a conjunction of actions and multiple approaches, simultaneously. Each form of action illuminates, nourishes and corrects the other. The experience of the WCC in helping to build up the capabilities of human rights organizations in Latin America, in close consultation with its member churches, amply demonstrated this principle. The pastoral, spiritual and moral support; the visits and missions; the exercise of political pressure through interventions with governments; the statements and positions made public; and the channelling of financial support at the level of institutions – all these instruments are valid and efficient only to the extent that they learn from and correct each other, and are applied together systematically. *Accompanhamento* includes all of these elements.

15. Maintain close ties with all the actors of international ecumenical solidarity. Consistent with the above, we deliberately underlined the importance of informing, visiting and involving all the actors across the ecumenical panorama with whom the WCC cooperated in strengthening human rights during that period in Latin America. Those actors outside Latin America included principally the WCC member churches in Europe and North America, but not exclusively, as well as their agencies. National councils of churches, their committees on refugees and those responsible for international affairs exchanged regular information with the WCC. Solid and frequent visits were made to those responsible for funding in church and government development agencies. Labour unions, student groups, people active in congregational life and members of parliament were encouraged to become involved in solidarity campaigns and actions. Credible and fresh information from human rights partners in Latin America, more often than not, proved more reliable than that from official sources. Such involvement enhanced the churches' abilities to critically inform their own governments about the situation and to pressure them from within, while coordinating with their leaders and with the WCC the common urgent action required.

Churches in each of these countries – from France to Norway to Canada, for example – were mobilized in their congregational life by the physical presence of Latin American refugees. The liturgical life of many local congregations was enriched to the extent that they gained insights from critical situations where Latin American communities – as in Central America – were faithful to their calling under persecution. For example, the spiritual and liturgical wealth shared by Latin American representatives during frequent encounters and services held in the Ecumenical Centre in Geneva, deeply affected and stimulated the staff of the WCC and its sister ecumenical and confessional organizations in the building.

In the final analysis the WCC's deliberate policy of encouraging full participation of the international ecumenical family in solidarity, greatly strengthened its mission of *acompanhamento* during the dark years of repression in Latin America.

10
What Are the Challenges Facing the Churches Today?

Thirty persons[1] met two years ago in Santiago de Chile, 20-23 October 2003, by invitation of the Social Aid Foundation of the Christian Churches (FASIC) and the WCC, with the aim of reflecting on the experiences of the churches and ecumenical organizations in Latin America during the dark years of military rule and repression. They came from Argentina, Brazil, Chile, Paraguay, Peru and Uruguay, accompanied by two persons from Canada and the USA. The Latin American Council of Churches (CLAI), the WCC, Church World Service from the USA and Kairos from Canada were officially represented. The title of the meeting, 'Latin America: Thirty Years of Ecumenical Commitment to Dignity and Human Rights' provided a fine opportunity to share the accumulated experience and work of the churches and organizations in these countries over the past thirty years. It also provided a clear opportunity to identify the challenges arising from the present social, economic and political realities of these countries.

The representative character of the meeting, with persons participating who had been closely involved in the pastoral and prophetic ministries of the churches during the dark years of repression and in the early days of the human rights organizations present, gives depth and weight to their conclusions. They are given below, in summary form.

The report of the group identifies these central challenges, addressed in three thematic areas: the action of the churches; human rights; and an ethic in the service of life.

The action of the churches
– We recognize that many churches joined in raising their voices to demand justice when the cries of victims and organizations had been

silenced. Nevertheless, not all the churches in our countries were in solidarity with the victims of violations and some sectors even collaborated with repression.

– We appreciate how churches played the role of 'sanctuary' as an expression of the Judeo-Christian tradition of protection, hospitality and healing.

– We appreciate the important role played by liturgy and celebration in the defence of life and we celebrate the churches' support of the people through worship services, prayer, vigils and other symbolic acts where solidarity and hope were strengthened.

– We realize today that many churches that were engaged in the past in actions of solidarity have lost this vocation of service and have come to concentrate more on the domestic concerns of their denominations.

– We observe that today churches are present in various ways in political life and in civil society, particularly in addressing issues of poverty and human rights.

Therefore we propose that:

1. The churches continue to deepen their theological reflection on the fresh challenges facing them, such as the decline in living standards and the increase in violence in the region.

2. The churches reflect on their practices and commitment in relation to dignity and human rights within the framework of their holistic mission and that they recover their vision of God as Lord of history.

3. The churches and ecumenical organizations continue to be 'sanctuaries', places of hospitality and solidarity for those who suffer: political and common-law prisoners, threatened and tortured by the judicial and prison systems; refugees, displaced persons and migrants; families separated as a result of the economic system; victims of discrimination, violence and exclusion. 'Churches as sanctuaries' for the defence of life and human rights, wherever they are threatened.

4. The churches and ecumenical organizations be more open to one another and strengthen the relationships between themselves as well as national, regional and world solidarity. They should work within the perspective of pastoral accompaniment, of exchange, of mutual commitment and the encouragement of different forms of encounter, such as, for example, participation in the World Social Forum.

5. The churches take upon themselves a commitment of citizenship, as an expression of their prophetic vocation against all forms of dis-

crimination, along with other actors in civil society, so as to contribute to the building of democracy, while maintaining their independence and faithfulness to the Gospel vis-à-vis the State and political parties. That, in this way, the churches contribute to a democratic vision in which the new form of genocide, resulting from the present political and economic model, can be condemned.

6. The churches, drawing equally upon the community traditions of the past and on the creativity of the present, seek liturgical forms that promote hope, life and resurrection as celebrations of their commitment.

The permanent challenge of human rights

– We recognize that during the last thirty years a new international situation has arisen, which is the context within which action for dignity and human rights in Latin America must take place. This new context is characterized by the end of the Cold War, by the consequent domination by one superpower in economic, political and military spheres, the increasingly visible gap between rich and poor countries, due to the widespread implementation of an economic model increasing inequality and weakening the democracies established after dictatorial regimes. New problems have emerged or come to the fore: hunger, poverty and high levels of unemployment and exploitation.

– We observe that in this new context an important agenda emerges, a product of the serious human rights violations and violations of the integrity of persons committed in the past, which no democracy can avoid and which our societies demand to see resolved.

– We appreciate the progress made, during the last thirty years, as the international community has become aware of the indivisibility, interdependence and solidarity of human rights, that is, civil and political rights with economic, social and cultural rights. We are convinced, out of the experience of our countries, that dignity can be infringed and life harmed, not only because of the violation of civil and political rights, but also through the denial of economic, social and cultural rights.

– We believe it necessary to emphasize the relevance of political involvement by the Organization of the American States and the United Nations within our national and regional contexts.

We think that the following themes should be given particular consideration:

1. Impunity and Memory

We reaffirm that impunity, in relation to human rights violations, is a factor undermining institutions in our societies and democracy itself. It is not only a violation of international norms and conventions that lay obligations upon our States. No amnesty should be an obstacle to justice. The recovery of memory is a duty that any society has towards itself. It involves keeping in mind events that have happened, so that the present can be understood, so that our future may be guided, so that the repetition of acts and of courses of action leading to tragedy and death can be avoided, and so that alternatives and values which have proved their capacity to build a different future can be affirmed.

2. Exclusion, Discrimination and Insecurity

We observe with concern that today's economic and social system produces exclusion and discrimination, depriving large and growing sectors of the wellbeing to which they are entitled. Special mention can be made of the impact of the system upon education and health, to which the majorities in our societies have limited or no access. Youth, women, migrants and refugees are particularly affected. In the same way, special attention should be paid to the discrimination suffered by indigenous peoples, as well as by those of African descent. Insecurity is a reality affecting the quality of daily life, degraded by violence on the part of individuals in public and private life.

3. Sustainable Development, External Debt and Care for the Environment

We consider it strategically urgent and important that our countries formulate coherent proposals for sustainable development that lead to overcoming poverty and hunger, leading to wellbeing without polluting or destroying our ecosystems. In this regard, the requirement that external debt be paid continues to hold back the possibility of wellbeing for our peoples, and, being a source of inequality, weakens our democracies yet further. We are, moreover, particularly concerned about the impact on the environment of so-called mega-projects.

Towards an ethic in the service of life

–   We affirm the absolute necessity of an ethic in the service of life – strict, supportive and responsible, as expressed by different religious confessions and by other, humanist, world views. We affirm our respect for, and our recognition of, the diverse world views that promote human dignity, justice and peace. We reject, therefore, 'ethical' positions based on the prevailing neo-liberal model that encourage individualism, consumerism and neglect of other people's needs. We also reject the use of religion to demonize, condemn and exclude people who are different.

– We affirm that reconciliation is the will of God, who desires fullness of life for all humankind, which is only partially achieved in history. We affirm that genuine reconciliation in societies that have experienced violent conflict can be achieved through a slow process that includes repentance, confession, a request for forgiveness from the perpetrator and reparation within a framework in which truth and justice prevail. We reject the false reconciliation that – motivated by selfish interests – denies knowledge of the whole truth and refuses legal action by proposing agreements that are a renewed attack on the dignity of the human person, especially the victims.

– We affirm the responsibility of the State to guarantee human security as an expression of the protection of all the rights of citizens. We reject the new reductionist attempts to reintroduce doctrines of internal and international security that violate the people's fundamental rights.

– We affirm the importance of International Law as expressed in declarations, treaties and conventions, as being the safeguard of human dignity, as well as the different international mechanisms with the same aim. We especially affirm the relevance of the Inter-American System of Human Rights as well as the establishment of the International Criminal Court, as an adequate instrument to respond to the most serious crimes against human rights.

– We affirm the close link between the *Oikoumene*, the expression of God's will that all humankind live in a common home, and International Law based on human rights and multilateralism, as universal norms for all human beings to live together.

We confess God the Creator, who reconciles us to God's very self and to one another by Jesus Christ. The Eucharist celebrates this reconciliation not only by remembering the past, but also by making Easter a present reality. The Eucharist teaches us the value of a Memory that again makes salvation a reality in history. We confess a God who looks with particular favour upon the poor and excluded. We affirm the important role that Liberation Theology has played during these thirty years and we recognize the need to deepen our present-day theological understanding, to take into account the new situation, particularly in relation to social, economic and environmental issues.

This new theological perspective will help us as Christians to interpret our experiences of memory, truth and justice in connection with the human rights violations in the region during the past thirty years that we have recalled in this encounter. Also, it will allow us to strengthen our prophetic commitment and political activity as we face new challenges.

NOTES

[1] Monseñor Alfonso Baeza D., President of the board of FASIC; Bishop Neftali Aravena, Vice-President of FASIC; José Burneo, of FEDEPAZ in Peru; Pastor Eduardo Cid, representing CLAI;   Pastor José de Luca, of MEDH, in Argentina; Pastor João Días de Araújo, of CEPS – the Ecumenical Commission for the Rights of the Earth, in Brazil; Bishop Aldo Etchegoyen, member of WCC's Central Committee, of the APDH in Argentina and CIEMAL, the Methodist regional body; William Fairbairn, of Kairos – Canadian Ecumenical Initiatives for Justice; Juan A. Gianotti, of SEDHU – Ecumenical Service for Human Dignity, in Uruguay; Teresa Gómez, of FASIC; Claudio González, of FASIC, Pastor Rafael Goto Silva, of the Christian Center of Promotion and Services, in Peru; the Rev. Charles Harper, for the WCC; Pastor Juan Armin Ihle, of IERP – the Evangelical Church of Rio de la Plata, in Uruguay; Rosa M. Lavecchia, representing Church World Service, USA; Guillermo Kerber, of the WCC, Enrique Pochat, of MEDH (from 1982-1997);   Marta Palma, of the WCC; Eliana Rolemberg, of CESE, in Brazil; Verónica Reyna, of FASIC; Héctor Salazar, of FASIC; Pastora Hilda Vence, of the Methodist Church of Uruguay; Cristina Vila, of CIPAE, in Paraguay; Christina T. Winnischofer, of the Anglican Episcopal Church of Brazil; the Rev. William Wipfler, of the NCCCUSA (1967-1988) and the Anglican Office, USA; Pastora Juana Albornoz, of the Committee of Protestant Evangelical Organizations, in Chile; and two supporting colleagues for the encounter, Mr. Hugo Villela, of AMERINDA, in Chile and Juan Salazar, of FASIC.

11

Conclusion: The Story of the Stale Bread

Images of the Latin American tragedy remain imprinted like flash photographs on the minds of people everywhere: Guido Rocha's sculpture, the Libertad Prison, the dance of the 'cueca sola', the lone vigil at the Plaza de Mayo, the dusty road to Emboscada, a Quechua braid, a presidential sword. They form part of a litany of detentions and disappearances, of torture, of waiting, that contributed to the new international levels of political apartheid that governments then practiced against their peoples. Today, poverty persists and the ranks of the marginalized are swelling.

On the other hand, the international community has discovered the strength of these people, as they have reasserted their history, resurrected their democratic traditions and called for justice and a new future. Symbols have become communicators of this other reality: that of the grandmothers working together; of book covers shouting 'Nunca Más!'; of impeccably dressed generals in the dock being sentenced for their crimes; of the power of the ballot box; of a non-violent and creative civil society, teeming with activists, advocates, militants, and the popular movements and associations that sprang up during the dark years of repression – and signs of renewed Christian communities, whose faith drove them to acts of solidarity.

This narrative will end with another story, with two symbols: that of the grey metallic doors of a prison and a piece of dried bread. I call it 'The Story of the Stale Bread'. The characters in the story are a group of women prisoners and a chaplain, the Methodist Bishop Aldo Etchegoyen. This is how he tells it...

Villa Devoto is a suburb of the city of Buenos Aires, very well known for its prison, which is one of the largest in the country. During the military government in Argentina, this prison had a special section for women who were suspected of having committed acts of subversion. There were some two hundred women held there. The military government had created a sentencing system that consisted of civil courts, military courts, and a third tier – prisoners 'at the disposal of the National Executive Authority'. There a three or five-year sentence could be commuted to one of many more years.

The prison system allowed only a Catholic chaplain to give pastoral care to the prisoners. A Protestant minister could obtain permission only in special circumstances to visit designated prisoners, who had submitted a request beforehand for a pastoral visit. Three women prisoners asked for a pastoral visit from me: Virginia, Mónica and María Celeste. After long negotiations, I was able to get permission to visit them. The military government was trying to keep in with the churches. It was about 1977. The repression was then at its height, hundreds of people were disappearing overnight, and those disappeared were being held in some three hundred secret centres and being tortured to extract information from them. I started to make weekly visits to the Villa Devoto Prison.

It would take me one hour to get there, another hour to show my credentials and be searched before being admitted, and then I had to wait before reaching the interview cubicles. I was given twenty minutes to speak with each of the three prisoners I was visiting. There were about one hundred interview cubicles located down a long narrow corridor. Each cubicle had a thick glass screen, though which you had to speak by means of a tube that enabled you to be heard on the other side. It was difficult to make yourself heard when there were many people visiting.

The great hope of these prisoners was to reach the end of their sentences: Mónica on 30 June 1980, Virginia and María Celeste on other dates. Days went by, and on the day when they were due for release... they continued to remain in custody for three further years by decision of the National Executive Authority. This system, together with the strict prison regime, was designed to break their spirit. Often prisoners did break down. It was a race to see who would snap first. The prisoners would shout out, 'I've got to get out of here!' The guards would shout back, 'We're going to destroy you!'

When Virginia was imprisoned she was pregnant. Her daughter Evita was born in prison and brought a little happiness, not only to her mother but also to all the women prisoners. Some months later the time came for Evita to be taken from her mother. You can imagine how desperate Virginia was, for at that time the military regime was making babies, and boys and girls, disappear, and then either giving them away or selling them on. In this case, happily, Evita was passed on to Virginia's parents, who lived in San Juan, 1,100 kilometres from Buenos Aires. About once a month they would come to visit Virginia in prison, and then, as Evita got older, they would bring her with them. Evita grew up seeing her mother only in the interview cubicle, and then only the upper half of her body. It was impossible for her to touch her or kiss her, as the thick glass stood between them. In her simple mind, her mummy was not a complete person, but a person with only half a body.

One day Mónica told me that they would like to share in a communion service. She had to ask for permission from the prison authorities for a personal contact visit, not in an interview cubicle. I thus wrote to the prison governor, who, after one month, replied that, according to the rules, only the Catholic chaplain could celebrate communion. After a few days, I wrote again, giving further reasons why Protestant prisoners should receive pastoral care from their own pastors. Permission was again refused. I insisted again, accusing the authorities of violating freedom of worship and of spiritually maltreating their prisoners. I received no reply, but, on my next visit, while I was being searched, they did indeed give me a reply – and a sharp one: I was not to trouble them any further on this matter, otherwise I would have much bigger problems... When I went home after this last attempt, I decided to keep the bread that I had saved for communion for another time when we would be able to celebrate communion together.

Years passed, and, finally, the military government fell and democracy was restored in Argentina in December 1983. On 1 December I received permission to celebrate communion with the three prisoners in the Villa Devoto Prison, which we did a few days before they were released. Before leaving home, I looked for the bread that I had kept years before – it was very meaningful for us. In the prison chapel we celebrated communion with that stale bread.

During the celebration, Virginia told me what she had experienced with Evita, who was then about six years old. She had also received permission for the first time for a personal visit from her family. On all previous visits over many years, they had only seen one another through the thick glass of the interview cubicle. Evita was radiant with joy and kept hugging her mother again and again. 'Are you happy, Evita?' asked her mother. 'Yes, Mama! I am very happy, because... you have got legs!'

When I returned home, I wrote:

Finally, permission was granted, and today we celebrated Holy Communion, but, after such a long wait, the bread had gone stale.

'Take, eat, this is my body.'

This was not the fresh soft bread of Sunday communion.

This was bread gone hard through years of waiting.

This was not the fresh bread of the congregation, but bread kept for years and gone stale.

This was not fresh bread, easy to break, but stale bread that was hard to break.

Stale bread of Holy Communion delayed,

Bread stale from long years of waiting,

Stale bread, symbolizing courage and resistance to armed might.

Bread, stronger than military repression,

Bread, full of meaning, which now feeds us in the faith, giving us abundant life.

Bread and wine of liberation,

Bread and wine of hope and freedom. Alleluia!

Appendix 1
Declaration on the Occasion
of the Fiftieth Anniversary of the Adoption
of the Universal Declaration of Human Rights,
Adopted by the Eighth Assembly
of the World Council of Churches,
Harare, Zimbabwe, 3-14 December 1998

PREAMBLE TO THE UNIVERSAL DECLARATION OF HUMAN RIGHTS ADOPTED BY THE THIRD GENERAL ASSEMBLY OF THE UNITED NATIONS, PARIS, 10 DECEMBER 1948

Whereas recognition of the inherent dignity and of the equal and inalienable rights of all members of the human family is the foundation of freedom, justice and peace in the world,

Whereas disregard and contempt for human rights have resulted in barbarous acts which have outraged the conscience of mankind, and the advent of a world in which human beings shall enjoy freedom of speech and belief and freedom from fear and want has been proclaimed as the highest aspiration of the common people,

Whereas it is essential, if man is not to be compelled to have recourse, as a last resort, to rebellion against tyranny and oppression, that human rights should be protected by the rule of law,

Whereas it is essential to promote the development of friendly relations between nations,

Whereas the peoples of the United Nations have in the Charter reaffirmed their faith in fundamental human rights, in the dignity and worth of the human person and in the equal rights of men and women and have determined to promote social progress and better standards of life in larger freedom,

Whereas Member States have pledged themselves to achieve, in cooperation with the United Nations, the promotion of universal respect for and observance of human rights and fundamental freedoms,

Whereas a common understanding of these rights and freedoms is of the greatest importance for the full realization of this pledge,

Now, *therefore*,

The General Assembly,

Proclaims this Universal Declaration of Human Rights as a common standard of achievement for all peoples and all nations, to the end that every individual and every organ of society, keeping this Declaration constantly in mind, shall strive by teaching and education to promote respect for these rights and freedoms and by progressive measures, national and international, to secure their universal and effective recognition and observance, both among the peoples of Member States themselves and among the peoples of territories under their jurisdiction.

DECLARATION OF THE EIGHTH ASSEMBLY OF THE WORLD COUNCIL OF CHURCHES

The first WCC Assembly in Amsterdam fifty years ago had high hopes for the Universal Declaration of Human Rights under discussion by the United Nations at that time. As we, representatives of churches in some 120 countries, gathered here in Harare on 10 December 1998 in the Eighth Assembly of the World Council of Churches, to reconsider the words of the Preamble, we find that they are as pertinent and challenging today as they were when they were adopted.

We remember with gratitude those who advocated on behalf of the ecumenical fellowship at the San Francisco Conference in 1945 the inclusion within the United Nations Charter of provisions for human rights, including a special Commission on Human Rights and Fundamental Freedoms to develop and implement guarantees for religious freedom and other rights.

We are thankful to those whose faith and vision contributed to the shaping and adoption of this common standard of achievement for all peoples and all nations. We remember those all around the world who have dedicated their lives to the further development of these rights, in order that there be a progressive subordination of force to the international rule of law.

We hear the cries of the victims of human rights violations, and feel their anger, frustrations, agony, loneliness, desperation and pain. We remember particularly those Christians and people of other faiths and convictions around the world who have suffered persecution and martyrdom in defense of human rights.

We recognize that in some languages the use of masculine terminology in the original wording of the Declaration would appear to exclude women. Nevertheless, women as well as men today find in the Declaration a foundation for their hopes and aspirations. The adoption of this Universal Declaration stands as one of the landmark achievements of humanity.

Most governments have now committed themselves to respect its provisions, but we are painfully aware that these principles have yet to receive universal observance and no country fully respects them. As a result of poverty, ignorance, exploitation and repression, very many people remain unaware that they are invested with such inalienable rights. More still are unable to exercise them.

As Christians, we believe that God created every person infinitely precious and endowed with equal dignity and rights. Yet we confess that we have often failed to respect such equality, even in our own midst. We have not always stood up courageously for those whose rights and human dignity are threatened or violated by discrimination, intolerance, prejudice and hatred. Indeed Christians have sometimes been agents of such injustice.

The World Council of Churches has affirmed that human rights, including the right to religious freedom, are not to be claimed by any religion, nation or group as an exclusive privilege, but rather that the enjoyment of these rights is essential in order to serve the whole of humanity. Yet we are aware that universal human rights have been repeatedly violated or misused in pursuit of particular religious, ideological, national, ethnic and racial interests.

In this Jubilee Assembly of the World Council of Churches held under the theme, "Turn to God – Rejoice in Hope", we continue to pursue the goal of unity for the Church and the whole of humankind.

We look forward with hope and reaffirm our faith that God will continue to guide us and give us strength to confront the potent forces of division, dehumanisation and social exclusion which assail us today.

In this spirit, we recommit ourselves to the principles of the Universal Declaration of Human Rights, and to promote and defend them in a way which takes into account:

♦ the values and insights into human rights and dignity derived from the rich heritage of peoples' religions, cultures and traditions;

♦ the rights of peoples, nations, communities and their cultures, as well as the rights of each individual within them;

♦ the indivisibility of human rights, including social, economic and cultural, civil and political rights, and the right to peace, to development and the integrity of the Creation;

♦ the right of every person and community, be they in the majority or in the minority, to participate fully in decisions about their common future;

♦ the equal rights of young and old, of children and adults, of women and men, and of all persons irrespective of their origin or condition.

We commit ourselves to pursue this goal in a way which does not further divide, but rather unites the human community through:

♦ encouraging and supporting the efforts of the United Nations;

♦ urging our governments to ratify and respect international and regional instruments for the promotion and protection of human rights, to monitor compliance with them in their own countries and around the world, and to underwrite that commitment with human and financial resources;

♦ seeking cooperation with peoples of other faiths and convictions;

♦ joining in partnerships with other civil society groups and organizations, and with governments and political authorities who share these aims.

This we do for the benefit of the present generation which desperately needs universal respect for and the exercise of the full range of human rights. We undertake these commitments especially for the children and youth of today, that they may take hope and claim the promise of the future. We do it so that the world in which we are among God's stewards will be passed on to future generations resting upon the firm foundations of freedom, justice and peace.

Appendix 2
Human Rights Organizations

NAMES OF THE ORGANIZATIONS OF THE LATIN
AMERICAN HUMAN RIGHTS MOVEMENT IN SOUTH AND
CENTRAL AMERICA, AND MEXICO WHICH THE WCC
ACCOMPANIED FROM 1970 TO 1990

SOUTHERN CONE AND BRAZIL

Argentina:
Comisión Argentina de Refugiados (CAREF)
Argentine Commission for Refugees
Asamblea Permanente por los Derechos Humanos (APDH)
Permanent Assembly for Human Rights
Abuelas de la Plaza de Mayo
Plaza de Mayo Grandmothers
Asociación Madres de Plaza de Mayo Línea Fundadora
Association of Plaza de Mayo Mothers' Founders' Line
Movimiento Ecuménico por los Derechos Humanos (MEDH)
Ecumenical Movement for Human Rights
Acción Popular Ecuménica (APE)
Ecumenical Popular Action
Fundación Ecuménica de Cuyo (FEC)
Ecumenical Foundation of Cuyo

Equipo Argentino de Antropología Forense (EAAF)
Argentine Forensic Anthropology Team
Centro de Orientación para la Vida Familiar (COVIFAC)
Orientation Centre for Family Life

Chile:
Comité Nacional de Refugiados (CONAR)
National Refugee Committee
Comité de Cooperación para la Paz en Chile (COPACHI)
Committee of Cooperation for Peace in Chile
Fundación de Ayuda Social de las Iglesias Cristianas (FASIC)
Social Assistance Foundation of the Christian Churches
Vicaria de la Solidaridad del Arzobispado (ICR) de Santiago
Vicariate of Solidarity of the Archbishopric of Santiago
Servicio Evangélico para el Desarrollo (SEPADE)
Protestant Development Service
Centro Ecuménico Misión Urbana Rural (CEMURI)
Ecumenical Centre for Urban-Rural Mission

Paraguay:
Mision de Amistad
Friendship Mission
Comité de Iglesias para Ayuda de Emergencias (CIPAE)
Churches' Committee for Emergency Aid
Comisión Nacional de Derechos Humanos
National Human Rights Commission
Banco Paraguayo de Datos (BPD)
Paraguayan Data Bank
Centro de Estudios Humanitarios (CEDHU)
Centre for Humanitarian Studies
Secretariado Internacional de Juristas por la Amnistía y la Democracia en Paraguay (SIJADEP)
International Jurists' Secretariat for Amnesty and Democracy in Paraguay

Uruguay:
Servicio Ecuménico de Reintegración (SER)/ Servicio de Rehabilitación Social (SERSOC)
Ecumenical Service for Reintegration / Social Rehabilitation Service

Servicio por la Paz y Justicia – Uruguay (SERPAJ)
Service for Peace and Justice – Uruguay
Centro Uruguay Independiente (CUI)
Independent Centre Uruguay
Instituto de Estudios Legales y Sociales del Uruguay (IELSUR)
Legal and Social Studies Institute of Uruguay
Secretariado Internacional de Juristas por la Amnistía en Uruguay (SIJAU)
International Secretariat of Jurists for Amnesty in Uruguay

Brazil:
Centro Ecumênico de Documentação e Informação (CEI / CEDI)
Ecumenical Centre for Documentation and Information
Coordinadora Ecumênica de Serviço (CESE)/Movimento Nacional de Direitos Humanos
Ecumenical Coordinating Service Group / National Human Rights Movement
Arquidiocese Metropolitana de São Paulo, Comissão Pastoral de Direitos Humanos e CLAMOR
Metropolitan Archdiocese of Sao Paulo, Human Rights Pastoral Commission and CLAMOR
Instituto de Ação Cultural (IDAC)
Institute of Cultural Action
Centro de Criação de Imagem Popular (CECIP)
Centre for the Creation of Popular Image
Movimento dos Trabalhadores Rurais Sem Terra (MST)
Landless Rural Workers Movement

ANDEAN REGION

Bolivia:
Asamblea Permanente por los Derechos Humanos en Bolivia (APDDHHB)
Permanent Assembly for Human Rights in Bolivia
Comité Impulsor de Juicio de Responsabilidad contra Luis García Meza y Colaboradores
Promotion Committee for Trial to determine Responsibility of Luis García Meza and Collaborators

Asociación de Familiares de Detenidos Desaparecidos y Mártires por la Liberación Nacional (ASOFAMD)
Association of Relatives of Disappeared Detainees and Martyrs for National Liberation

Ecuador:
Comisión Ecuménica de Derechos Humanos (CEDHU)
Ecumenical Human Rights Commission
Centro de Educación Popular CEDIS – CEDEP
Popular Education Centre

Peru:
Centro de Estudios y Acción para la Paz (CEAPAZ)
Centre for Study and Action for Peace
Coordinadora Nacional de Derechos Humanos
National Coordinating Committee for Human Rights
Asociación Pro-Derechos Humanos (APRODEH)
Association for Human Rights
Comisión Nacional de Derechos Humanos (CONADEH/COMISEDH)
National Commission for Human Rights
Comisión Paz y Esperanza del Consejo Nacional Evangélico de Peru (CONEP)
Peace and Hope Commission of the National Protestant Council of Peru
Comisión Andina de Juristas
Andean Commission of Jurists

Colombia:
Centro de Investigación y de Educación Popular (CINEP)
Research and Popular Education Centre
Grupo de Enlace con los Comités Colombia en el Exterior
Liaison Group with Colombian Committees Abroad

Venezuela:
Centro Evangélico Venezolano por la Justicia (CEVEJ)
Venezuelan Protestant Centre for Justice
Programa Venezolano de Educación y Acción en Derechos Humanos (PROVEA)
Venezuelan Programme for Education and Action on Human Rights

CENTRAL AMERICA AND MEXICO

Costa Rica:
Departamento Ecuménico de Investigación (DEI)
Ecumenical Department of Research
Instituto Interamericano de Derechos Humanos (IIDH)
Interamerican Human Rights Institute
Comité Ecuménico Pro Derechos Humanos (CEPRODHU)
Ecumenical Committee for Human Rights
Comisión para la Defensa de los Derechos Humanos en Centroamérica (CODEHUCA)
Commission for the Defence of Human Rights in Central America

El Salvador:
Asociación Bautista de El Salvador y la Iglesia Bautista Emanuel
Baptist Association of El Salvador and the Emmanuel Baptist Church
Departamento de Derechos Humanos de la Iglesia Luterana en El Salvador
Human Rights Department of the Lutheran Church in El Salvador
Comité Ecuménico de Ayuda Humanitaria (CEAS)
Ecumenical Humanitarian Aid Committee
Socorro Juridíco Cristiano
Christian Legal Aid
Oficina de Tutela Legal del Arzobispado de San Salvador
Legal Defence Office of the Archbishopric of San Salvador
Comisión de Derechos Humanos de El Salvador
Human Rights Commission of El Salvador

Guatemala:
Comité Pro-Justicia y Paz de Guatemala
Committee for Justice and Peace in Guatemala
Comisión Guatemalteca de Derechos Humanos (CDDHH)
Guatemalan Human Rights Commission
Grupo de Derechos Humanos de Guatemala (CDHG)
Human Rights Group of Guatemala

Honduras:
Comisión de Desarrollo y Emergencias (CODE)
Development and Emergencies Commission

Comité para la Defensa de los Derechos Humanos en Honduras (CODEH)
Committee for the Defence of Human Rights in Honduras
Centro Ecuménico Regional Centroamericano (CERCA)
Central American Regional Ecumenical Centre

Nicaragua:
Asociación Nicaragüense Pro Derechos Humanos (ANPDH)
Nicaraguan Association for Human Rights
Bufete Legal de la Iglesia Morava de Nicaragua
Legal Assistance Office of the Moravian Church of Nicaragua
Centro Nicaraguense de Derechos Humanos (CENIDH)
Nicaraguan Human Rights Centre
Comisión Nacional de Promoción y Protección de los Derechos Humanos (CNPPDH
National Commission for Promotion and Protection of Human Rights
Comisión Permanente de Derechos Humanos de Nicaragua (CPDH)
Permanent Human Rights Commission of Nicaragua
Comité Evangélico pro-Ayuda al Desarrollo (CEPAD)
Protestant Committee for Development Aid

Panamá:
Programa de Derechos Humanos de las Iglesias Luterana y Metodista (HAPP/IEMPA)
Human Rights Programme of the Lutheran and Methodist Churches

Mexico:
Centro de Promoción y Defensa de los Derechos Humanos "Fr. Francisco de Vitoria, O.P."
Centre for the Promotion and Defence of Human Rights "Father Francisco de Vitoria, O.P."

REGIONAL LATIN AMERICA

Consejo Latinoamericano de Iglesias (CLAI)
Latin American Council of Churches

Pastoral de Consolación y Solidaridad (CLAI)
Pastoral Programme of Consolation and Solidarity of the Latin American Council of Churches
Iglesia y Sociedad en América latina (ISAL)
Latin America Commission on Church and Society
Movimiento de Estudiantes Cristianos (MEC)
Student Christian Movement
Unión Latino Americana de Juventud Evangélica (ULAJE)
Latin American Union of Protestant Youth
Comisión Evangélica Latinoamericana de Educación Cristiana (CELADEC)
Latin American Protestant Christian Education Commission
Federación Latinoamericana de Asociaciónes de Familiares de Detenidos-Desaparecidos (FEDEFAM) y sus afiliados en Argentina, Bolivia, Brasil, Colombia, Chile, Ecuador, El Salvador, Guatemala, Honduras, Mexico, Nicaragua, Paraguay, Peru and Uruguay
Latin American Federation of Associations of Relatives of the Detained-Disappeared Persons, and its affiliates
Servicio por la Paz y Justicia (SERPAJ) – América latina
Service for Peace and Justice in Latin America

REGIONAL CARIBBEAN

Caribbean Conference of Churches
Caribbean Rights

CARIBBEAN NATIONAL PARTNERS

Jamaica Council of Human Rights
Guyana Human Rights Association
Centre Oecuménique des Droits Humains (CEDH), Haiti
Ecumenical Human Rights Centre, Haiti
Program of Renewal and Social Investigation for Action (PRISA) – Puerto Rico
Instituto Puertorriqueño de Derechos Civiles (IPDC)
Puerto Rican Civil Rights Institute
Proyecto Caribeño para Justicia y Paz
Caribbean Project for Justice and Peace
Comité de Trabajo Ecuménico Dominicano (COTEDO)
Dominican Ecumenical Working Committee

Appendix 3
Bibliography of Selected Reading

The publications listed below shed a strong light on the heavy period of repression affecting Latin American societies under authoritarian rule from the 1960s to the 1990s. The list is far from exhaustive, given the great number of testimonies, reports and historical analyses which have appeared in recent years regarding human rights violations perpetrated during this period. It is the hope of the author that the following selection of published material will help the reader to further understand, from a Christian ecumenical perspective, the detailed nature and scale of human rights violations which occurred during that time. Many churches and Christian communities in Latin America, working together and associated with the world ecumenical family, were actors fully engaged in the struggle for the defence of life and human dignity. Several of these works were written by persons or groups intimately acquainted with detention, torture, or martyrdom. The book titles marked with an asterisk* designate publications produced by local ecumenical human rights groups with support from the World Council of Churches.

General:
América Latina: Treinta Años de Compromiso Ecuménico con la Dignidad y los Derechos Humanos (Encuentro auspiciado por el Consejo Mundial de Iglesias y la Fundación de Ayuda Social de las Igle-

sias Cristianas – FASIC, en Santiago de Chile, 20-23 de octubre de 2003).

Dussel, Enrique, *A History of the Church in Latin America: Colonialism to Liberation (1492-1979).* Translated and revised by Alan Neely from the third edition of *Historia de la Iglesia en América latina.* (Grand Rapids, Michigan, USA: Wm. B. Eerdmans Publishing Company, 1981)

Forms of Solidarity : Human Rights – proceedings of a seminar held at the International Reformed Centre John Knox, 14-25 August, 1987 (Geneva, John Knox Series, 1988)

Derechos Humanos y Democracia: la contribución de las Organizaciones no Gubernamentales. Frühling E., Hugo, coordenador.Vários autores (Santiago de Chile: para el Instituto Interamericano de Derechos Humanos, 1991).

Gelber, George, ed. *Poverty and Power: Latin America After 500 Years* (London: CAFOD, 1992)

Hayner, Priscilla B., *Unspeakable Truths: Facing the Challenge of Truth Commissions* (New York, London: Routledge, 2002)

Higgins, Martha, *Political Policing: the United States and Latin America* (Durham and London: Duke University Press, 1998)

Lernoux, Penny, *Cry of the People* (Garden City, New York: Doubleday and Company, Inc., 1980)

Signos de Lucha y Esperanza: testimonios de la Iglesia en América latina 1973-1978 (Lima: Centro de Estudios y Publicaciones – CEP, 1978) y *Signos de Vida y Fidelidad: Testimonios de la Iglesia en América Latina 1978-1982* (CEP, 1983)

Verdad y Reconciliación:Reflexiones Éticas: Ponencias presentadas en el Seminario realizado en Lima en octubre de 2001. Autores: Salomón Lerner, José Burneo, Guillermo Kerber, Pilar Coll, Rafael Goto, Xabier Etxeberria, Felipe Zegarra, Francisco Moreno R., Federico Pagura, Dario López y Tony Mifsud. Encuentro auspiciado por el Consejo Mundial de Iglesias (CMI) y organizado por la Fundación Ecuménica para el Desarrollo y la Paz (FEDEPAZ), el Concilio Nacional Evangélico del Perú (CONEP), el Consejo Latinoamericano de Iglesias (CLAI), el Instituto Bartolomé de las Casas (IBC) y el Centro de Estudios y Publicaciones (CEP). (Lima: Ediciones CEP, 2001)*

Verdad, Justicia y Reparación: Desafíos para la democracia y la convivencia social. Autores: Carlos Martín Beristain, Patricia Tappatá de Valdez (Argentina), Andrés Dominguez Vial (Chile), Benjamin Cuéllar Martinez (El Salvador), Helen Beatriz Mack Chang (Guatemala) y Rolando Ames Cobián (Peru). Prefacio por Massimo Tommasoli y Roberto Cuéllar M. (Stockholm y San José : Instituto Internacional para la Democracia y la Asistencia Electoral IDEA y Instituto Interamericano de Derechos Humanos IIDH, 2005). En anexo, un CD-ROM con informaión detallada de cada caso indicado arriba.

WCC publications:

Sabanes Plou, Dafne, "Latin America", in *A History of the Ecumenical Movement, Volume 3, 1968-2000*, edited by John Briggs, Mercy Amba Oduyoye and Georges Tsetsis (Geneva: WCC, 2004). pp. 565-589

The Churches in International Affairs: Reports 1974-1978, 1979-1982, 1983-1986, 1987-1990, 1991-1994, 1995-1998 (Geneva, CCIA – The Commission of the Churches on International Affairs of the WCC)

Harper, Charles, ed. *Impunity: An Ethical Perspective: Six case studies from Latin America* (Geneva: WCC Publications, 1986) y traducción del ingles en *Impunidad: una perspectiva ética: seis estudios de casos de América Latina* (Montevideo: Ediciones Trilce, 1996)

Jacques, Geneviève, *Beyond Impunity: an Ecumenical Approach to Truth, Justice and Reconciliation* (Geneva: WCC, 2000) y traducción del inglés en: *Más allá de la impunidad: un enfoque ecuménico de la verdad, la justicia y la reconciliación* (Ginebra, WCC Publications, 2001)

Weingärtner, Erich, *Human Rights on the Ecumenical Agenda* (Geneva: CCIA Background Information Series,1983)

Argentina:

Cohen Salama, Mauricio, *Tumbas Anonimas: Informe sobre la identificación de restos de víctimas de la represión ilegal.* Equipo Argentino de Antropología Forense (Buenos Aires: Catálogos Editora, 1992)

Entre el Dolor y la Esperanza: Jornada por los Derechos Humanos: Acto realizado por el MEDH durante la 37a. Reunión del Comité Central del Consejo Mundial de Iglesias, en Buenos Aires 28 de julio al 8 de agosto 1985 (Buenos Aires: Ediciones del Movimiento Ecuménico por los Derechos Humanos, MEDH, 1985)

Nunca Más: Informe de la Comisión Nacional Sobre la Desaparicón de Personas (CONADEP), y Anexos del Informe de la CON-

ADEP. Prologo por Ernesto Sábato. (Buenos Aires: Editorial Universitaria de Buenos Aires, 1984). Accesible sur la página web < www.nuncamas.org/index.htm >

Nunca Más: The Report of the Argentine National Commission on the Disappeared, (First published in Great Britain by Faber and Faber Ltd, 1986, New York: Farrar Straus Giroux, 1986, in association with Index on Censorship, London)

Fisher, Jo, *Mothers of the Disappeared* (London: Zed Books Ltd, Boston: South End Press, 1989)

Verbitsky, Horacio, *El Vuelo* (Buenos Aires: Grupo Editorial Planeta, 1995)

La Desaparición Forzada como Crimen de Lesa Humanidad: Coloquio de Buenos Aires 10 al 13 de octubre de 1988. Organizado por el Grupo de Iniciativa para una Convención contra las Desapariciones Forzadas de Personas. Prólogo por Jorge Novak, Obispo de Quilmes (Buenos Aires: Paz Producciones, 1989).

Lopez, Mauricio Amilcar, *Los Cristianos y el Cambio Social en la Argentina: Programa Histórico Social 1965-1975, Tomos I y II.* Presentación por Oscar Bracelis; Introducción, *"Mauricio Lopez : Homo Oecumenicus"* por Julio de Santa Ana (Mendoza: Acción Popular Ecuménica y Fundación Ecuménica de Cuyo, 1989)*

Restitución de niños: Abuelas de Plaza de Mayo. Prólogo por Estela Barnes de Carlotto, Presidente; Introducción por Alicia Lo Giúdice (Buenos Aires: Editorial Universitaria de Buenos Aires, 1997)

Bolivia:

Acusación a la Dictadura del Narcotráfico, vários autores; auspiciado y organizado por la Asociación de Familiares de Detenidos Desaparecidos y Mártires por la Liberación Nacional (ASOFAMD). (La Paz: Ediciones Gráficas, 1993)

Aguiló, Federico, *"Nunca Mas" Para Bolivia* (Cochabamba: Colorgraf Rodríguez, 1993)

Calderón, F y Dandler, J, compiladores, *Bolivia : la fuerza histórica del campesinado* (La Paz: : Centro de Estudios de la Realidad Económica y Social y Ginebra, Suiza: Instituto de Investigaciones de las Naciones Unidas para el Desarrollo Social, 1986)

Camargo Crespo, Artemio, *Cronología de una resistencia : Julio 1980, Mina "Siglo XX", Bolivia/Journal de la résistance: Juillet 1980...* (Genève, Suisse: Editions Centre Europe-Tiers Monde – CETIM, 1982)

Espinal Camps, Luis, *El Grito de Un Pueblo* (La Paz: Asamblea Permanente de los Derechos Humanos en Bolivia (APDHB) y Lima, Perú: Centro de Estudios y Publicaciones (CEP), 1981

Paz Claros, Iván, ed., *Juicio de responsabilidad contra Luis García Meza y sus colaboradores* (Sucre, La Paz, Bolivia: Ediciones Gráficas "E.G.", Junio de 1993).*

Tierra de dolor y esperanza: Testimonios Bolivia 1976-81. Selección y elaboración por Mujica, L. (Lima, Perú: Centro de Estudios y Publicaciones (CEP), 1981

Brazil:

Brasil Nunca Mais: Um Relato para a História. Com prefácios do Cardeal-Arcebispo de São Paulo, Paulo Evaristo Arns e do ex-Secretário-Geral do Conselho Mundial de Igrejas, Dr. Philip Potter. (Petrópolis, RJ: Editora Vozes Ltda., 1985)*

Dossiê dos Mortos e Desaparecidos Políticos a Partir de 1964. Publicado juntamente com a Comissão de Familiares de Mortos e Desaparecidos Políticos e o Instituto de Estudo da Violência do Estado – IEVE. e o Grupo Tortura Nunca Mais de Pernambuco (ver Annexo bibliográfico abaixo) (Recife: Companhia Editora de Pernambuco, 1995 / São Paulo: Imprensa Oficial do Governo do Estado de São Paulo, 1996).

Gaspari, Elio, *A Ditadura Escancarada.* Sobre os Anos de Chumbo – 1969 a 1974. (São Paulo: Editora Schwarcz Ltda., 2002). Segundo volume numa série de cinco.

Lima, Samarone, *CLAMOR: A Vitória de uma Conspiração Brasileira* (Rio de Janeiro: Editora Objetiva Ltd., 2003).

Projeto Brasil Nunca Mais, 6891 pp., 12 volúmenes de la história de la represión en el Brasil bajo los gobiernos militares: Tomo I: *O Regime Militar*; Tomo II, vol. 1: *A Pesquisa*, vol 2: *Os Atingidos*, vol. 3: *Os Funcionários*; Tomo III: *Perfil dos Atingidos* (también publicado como separata por Editora Vozes, 1988); Tomo IV: *As Leis Repressivas*; Tomo V, vol.1: *A Tortura*, vol.2 y 3: *As Torturas*, vol.4: *Os Mortos*; Tomo VI, vol.1: *Índices dos Anexos*, vol.2: *Inventário dos Anexos*. (São Paulo: publicado por la Arquidiócesis de São Paulo, 1985).* Accesible para consulta en el Centro de Documentação e Informação Científica (CEDIC) de la Pontifícia Universidade Católica de São Paulo (PUC-SP) como también en la biblioteca del Consejo Mundial de Iglesias, Ginebra, Suiza. This collection is available for consultation at the Library of the WCC, as well as at CEDIC/PUC-SP.

(see Appendix I, List of Archives, Brasil, item 6). The entire archive of documentation – over one million pages – which formed the basis of these twelve volumes, as well as of the book *Brasil Nunca Mais*, is found in the CEDIC centre referred to above.

Rocha, Jan, *Brazil: A Guide to the People, Politics and Culture* (London: Latin America Bureau, (Research and Action, Ltd. & Brooklyn, NY: Interlink Books, 1997)

Torture in Brazil: A Shocking Report on the Pervasive Use of Torture by Brazilian Military Governments, 1964-1979. Translated from the original *Brasil Nunca Mais* by Jaime Wright; edited with a new preface by Dassin, J. (Austin, Texas: University of Texas Press, 1998). A first edition was published under the title *Torture in Brazil: A report by the Archdiocese of São Paulo* (New York: Random House Vintage books, 1986) forwarded by Paulo Evaristo, Cardinal Arns, the Archbishop of São Paulo and Philip Potter, General Secretary of the WCC, 1972-1984.

Weschler, Lawrence, *A Miracle, A Universe: Settling Accounts with Torturers*, with a new Postscript (Chicago, London: The University of Chicago Press Edition, 1998). Originally published 1990 by Pantheon Books, a division of Random House, New York.

The original English edition translated into Portuguese by Tomás Rosa Bueno and Celso Nogueira as *Um Milagre, Um Universo: O Acerto de Contas com os Torturadores* (São Paulo, Editora Schwarcz Ltda., 1990)

Chile:

20 Años de historia de la Agrupación de Familiares de Detenidos Desaparecidos de Chile: un camino de imágines (Santiago: Corporación Agrupación de Familiares…,1997)

Chile: Memoria Prohibida: las Violaciones a los Derechos Humanos 1973 – 1983. Tomos I – III. Texto por Atria, Rodrigo. Autores: Ahumada, E.; Egaña, J.L.; Góngora, A.; Quesney,C.; Saball, G. y Villalobos, G. (Santiago de Chile: Pehuén Editores, 1989)*

¿Donde Estan? Tomos I-VII. Antecedentes relativos a casos de detenidos-desaparecidos en Chile, 1899 páginas. (Santiago de Chile: Vicaría de la Solidaridad del Arzobispado de Santiago, 1978-1979)

Exilio: 1986 / 1978, por Varios Autores: T. Gomez, V. Rogazzy *et al*; Introducción por Obispo Isaías Gutiérrez V. de la Iglesia Metodista de Chile, Obispo Auxiliar Jorge Hourton P. de la Iglesia Católica, Pastor Stefan Schaller de la Iglesia Evangélica Luterana en Chile y Claudio González U., Secretario General de la Fundación de Ayuda Social de las Iglesias Cristianas – FASIC (Santiago de Chile: Amerinda Ediciones, 1986)

Garcés, Mario / Nicholls, Nancy, *Para una Historia de los DD.HH. en Chile: Historia Institucional de la Fundación de Ayuda Social de las Iglesias Cristianas* FASIC 1975-1991 (LOM Ediciones/ FASIC, Santiago de Chile, 2005)

Kornbluh, Peter, *The Pinochet File: A Declassified Dossier on Atrocity and Accountability* (New York, London: The New Press, 2003)

Precht Bañados, Padre Cristián, *En la Huella del Buen Samaritano: Breve História de la Vicaría de la Solidaridad* (Santiago de Chile: Editorial Tiberíades, 1998)

Informe de la Comisión Nacional de Verdad y Reconciliación. Accesible en < www.derechoschile.com/espanol/rettig.htm >

Report of the Chilean National Commission on Truth and Reconciliation, Volumes 1 and 2. Translated by Phillip E. Berryman, with an introduction by José Zalaquett. (Notre Dame, Indiana, USA and London: Center for Civil and Human Rights, Notre Dame Law School, University of Notre Dame Press, 1993). Accessible on < www.derechoschile.com/english/rettig.htm >

Trauma, Duelo y Reparación: una experiencia de trabajo psicosocial en Chile. Un aporte colectivo. Edición preparada por la FASIC (Santiago: Editorial Interamericano Ltda., 1987)*

Tyndale, Wendy, *Chile Under the Military Regime*, with a forward by Lord Ramsey of Canterbury. (London: Chile Committee for Human Rights, 1975)

Verdugo, Patricia, *Interferencia Secreta: 11 de Septiembre de 1973* (Santiago de Chile: Editorial Sudamericana Chilena, 1998)

Paraguay:

Aquino, Olda Caballero, *Por Orden Superior*, with a prologue by Esther Prieto (Asunción: Ñanduti Vive / Intercontinental Editora, 1989

El Precio de la Paz, Coordinador: José M. Blanch S.J. with prefaces by Ismael Rolón, archbishop emeritus of Asunción, Theo van Boven, former chairman of the Commission of the Churches on International Affairs of the WCC, and others. (Asunción: Ediciones Centro de Estudios Paraguayos "Antonio Guasch" – CEPAG, 1991)*

En los Sótanos de los Generales: los Documentos Ocultos del Operativo Condor, por Alfredo Boccia Paz, Miguel H. López, Antonio V. Pecci y Gloria Giménez Guanes (Asunción, Paraguay: Expolibro, Servilibro, 2002)

Peru:

El informe final de la comisión de la verdad y reconciliación del Perú. Accesible en : < www.cverdad.org.pe >

Gutíerrez, Tomás, *Evangélicos, Democracia y Nueva Sociedad* (Lima: Editorial Línea Andina S.A.C., 2005)

Poole, Deborah & Rénique, Gerardo, *Peru: Time of Fear*, (London: Latin America Bureau, 1992)

Responsabilidad Internacional del Estado Peruano: el Caso Alegría y Otros ante la Corte Interamericana de Derechos Humanos. *Presentación por Iván Bazán Chacón (Lima: Fundación Ecuménica para el Desarrollo y la Paz – FEDEPAZ, 1997)*

Uruguay:

Aguirre, Luis Pérez, *Si Digo Derechos Humanos...* (Montevideo: Servicio Paz y Justicia – SERPAJ, 1991)

Delmonte, Carlos, *Un Gramo de Locura...* Prólogo por Graciela Fernández Meijide. (Buenos Aires: Asociación Ediciones La Aurora,1988)

Silva, Alberto, *Perdidos en el Bosque* (Montevideo: Familiares de Uruguayos Detenidos/Desaparecidos, 1989)

Uruguay Nunca Mas: Informe Sobre la Violación a los Derechos Humanos 1972-1985 (Montevideo: Servicio Paz y Justicia Uruguay,1989)

Uruguay Nunca Más: Human Rights Violations, 1972-1985 (translated from the original Spanish by Elizabeth Hampsten), Servicio Paz y Justicia – Uruguay (Philadelphia, Pa, USA: Temple University Press, 1989)

Appendix 4
Current Archives on Human Rights
in Latin America

1. Current archives in the World Council of Churches (WCC)
The classified records of the Human Rights Resources Office for Latin America (HRROLA) are located in the WCC archives. They contain detailed correspondence with churches and human rights organizations, reports of delegations and missions, institutional minutes, records of actions taken, communications, testimonies and publications related to the Council's cooperation with churches and groups in Latin America in the defence and promotion of human rights from 1970 to 1990. The contents can be consulted on-line at: http://library.wcc-coe.org

Inquiries may be addressed to:
WCC Library
Route de Ferney 150
P.O. Box 2100
CH-1211 Geneva 2
SWITZERLAND

Telephone: +41 (22) 7916279
Telefax : +41 22 7102022
E-mail : library@wcc-coe.org

2. Current archives located in Latin America

The most important detailed documentation on human rights violations has been organized, in recent years, within each country where they occurred. Listed below are some of the main archives and centres of documentation containing primary data and secondary material accessible to researchers and to the public. The author expresses his deep gratitude to the following persons for their active cooperation with him in collecting and providing the valuable archival information, listed below. Several are esteemed friends and partners with the WCC in human rights advocacy in the various countries cited.

We are particularly grateful to Walther Albarracin (Bolivia), Judith Aranciba, (Bolivia), Rodolfo M. Aseretto (Paraguay), Laura Bálsamo (Uruguay), Arturo Blatezky (Argentina), José Burneo (Peru), Roberto Cuellar (Costa Rica), Aldo Etchegoyen (Argentina), Elza Ferreira Lobo (Brasil), Yuri Gahona (Chile), Hugo García (Argentina), Claudio González (Chile), Ingrid Jaschek (Argentina), Anabel Lotko (Argentina), Lucrecia Molina Theissen (Costa Rica), Ivan Paz Claros (Bolivia), Eliana Rolemberg (Brasil), Patricia Tappatá de Valdez (Argentina), Cristina Vila (Paraguay), José Zalaquett (Chile), Cristina Zeledon (Costa Rica), and to their dedicated colleagues.

ARCHIVES AND/OR DOCUMENTATION CENTRES
IN LATIN AMERICA HOLDING INFORMATION
AND DOCUMENTATION ON VIOLATIONS,
REPORTS MADE, AND SUPPORT GIVEN
IN THE FIELD OF HUMAN RIGHTS:

I. SOUTHERN CONE REGION AND BRAZIL

ARGENTINA

1. Comisión Argentina de Refugiados (CAREF) *(Argentinian Commission for Refugees)*
Contents of the archives: Records on refugees up to 1980. Documentation of the Office in Solidarity with Argentinian Exiles.
E-mail address: caref@caref.org.ar

2. Movimiento Ecumenico por los Derechos Humanos (MEDH) *(Ecumenical Movement for Human Rights)*
Contents of the archives: Historical archive on the terrorist state that brought ruin to Argentina from 1976 onwards, its consequences, the economic, social and political genocide and the resistance of the people.
Postal address: Moreno 1785 1° Piso, C 1093 ABG Ciudad de Buenos Aires
E-mail address: comunicacion@medh.org.ar, educacion@medh.org.ar

3. Asamblea Permanente por los Derechos Humanos (APDH) *(Permanent Assembly for Human Rights)*
Contents of the archives: Reports on persons who had disappeared and been detained. Documentation on institutions. Press archive and documentation centre.
Postal address: Avda. Callao 569 3 cuerpo 1 piso. Ciudad de Buenos Aires
E-mail address: apd@apdh-argentina.org.ar
Web page: www.apdh-argentina.org.ar

4. Servicio Paz y Justicia (SERPAJ) *(Peace and Justice Service)*
Contents of the archives: Information on ecumenical work from 1973 to the present day. Documentation of the Technical Commission and human rights organizations for 1982/83. Documentation centre from 1990 containing journalistic and ecumenical documentation.
Postal address: Piedras 753; Ciudad de Buenos Aires
E-mail address: serpaj@serpaj.org.ar

5. Asociación Madres de Plaza de Mayo Línea Fundadora *(Association of Plaza de Mayo Mothers, Founder's Line)*
Contents of the archives: Documentation on its own activities and photo archive. Journalistic archive, updated from 1986. Archive on institutions from 1986 onwards. Participant in Memoria Abierta (Open Memory), which is a group of human rights organizations holding information on historical documentation.
Postal address: Piedras 153 1° A; Ciudad de Buenos Aires
E-mail address: madreslineafundadora@aolsinectis.com.ar
Web page: www.madreslineafundadora.org.ar

6. Abuelas de Plaza de Mayo *(Plaza de Mayo Grandmothers)*
Contents of the archives: Reports on children disappeared and born in custody. Press cuttings. Documentaion on institutions.
Postal address: Virrey Ceballos 592 PB 1; Ciudad de Buenos Aires
E-mail address: abuelas@abuelas.org.ar
Web pages: www.abuelas.org.ar / www.redporlaidentidad.org.ar
www.conadis.jus.gov.ar

7. Asociación de Ex Detenidos Desaparecidos *(Association of former detainees and disappeared)*
Contents of the archives: Concentration camps. Lists of victims seen and their victimizers.
Postal address: Carlos Calvo 1780, Depto 10, C1102ABJ, Ciudad de Buenos Aires
E-mail address: aedd@exdesaprecidos.org.ar

8. Asociación de Familiares de Detenidos y Desaparecidos por Razones Políticas *(Association of Relatives of Persons Detained and Disappeared for Political Reasons)*
Contents of the archives: Statements on reports of persons detained/ disappeared. Photographic archive, posters, institutional documenta-

tion and mail. Artistic work by detainees. Periodicals. Archives of court prodceedings. Data base of persons detained/disappeared.
Postal address: Río Bamba 34; Ciudad de Buenos Aires
E-mail address: faderap@fibertel.com.ar

9. Equipo Argentino de Antropología Forense *(Argentinian Forensic Anthropology Team)*
Contents of the archives: Written archives and statements from various sources on persons disappeared during the last Argentinian military dictatorship, for the purpose of recovering and indentifying their remains.
Postal address: Avda. Rivadavia 2443; 2do piso 3 y 4 ; Ciudad de Buenos Aires C1034acd
E-mail address: eaaf@velocom.com.ar

10. Centro de Estudios Legales y Sociales (CELS) *(Legal and Social Study Centre)*
Contents of the archives: Participates in the Memoria Abierta (Open Memory) project (see below).
Postal address: Piedras 543; Ciudad de Buenos Aires
E-mail address: cels@cels.org.ar

11. Archivos del Estado: Secretaría de Derechos Humanos de la Nación (Archivo Nacional de la Memoria) *(State Archives: National Secretariat for Human Rights (National Memory Archive))*
Contents of the archives: Archive of the *National Commission on the Disappearance of Persons (CONADEP)*: computerized archives of reports of disappeared persons. It is kept permanently updated. Computerized archives of legal proceedings and compensation laws for prisoners and persons disappeared or deceased.
Postal address: 25 de mayo 544 2° piso.; Ciudad de Buenos Aires
E-mail address: anm@derhuman.jus.gov.ar

12. Comisión Provincial por la Memoria/ Dirección de Inteligencia de la Policia de la Provincia de Buenos Aires (DIPBA) *(Provincial Commission for Remembering/ Intelligence Branch of the Police of the Province of Buenos Aires)*
Contents of the archives: The DIPBA archive is an extensive and detailed record of the political ideological persecution of men and women over half a century. Surveillance and card-indexing were its main functions from its creatiion in 1957 until its abolition in 1998. In

2001, under Law 12.642, it was passed to the Provincial Memory Commission. From October 2003, the Archive is available for consultation by individuals (mainly victims and those directly affected by the miliary dictatorships) and persons engaged in research. The archive contains intelligence reports giving information on events, organizations and individuals, arising from the field work of the police stations in Buenos Aires. The intelligence reports are accompanied by a complete record of the press coverage, local, provincial and national, for each outstanding event in national political life and for each organization.

Postal address: Calle 54, N° 487, entre 4 y 5 (1900) La Plata
E-mail address: cmemoria@speedy.com.ar
Web page: www.comisionporlamemoria.org

BRAZIL

1. Centro de Documentação e Informação Científica (CEDIC) *(Documentation and Scientific Information Centre of the Pontifical Catholic University of São Paulo (PUC-SP))*
Contents of the archives: It possesses the record of **CLAMOR** (documentation from 1977 to 1991) on repression in the Southern Cone (periodicals, dossiers on disappearances of children, correspondence and press cuttings). These are still being processed. The archives of the **Brasil Nunca Mais** project were presented to the PUC-SP by Dom Paulo Evaristo Arns and are also held in this Documentation and Scientific Information Centre (CEDIC).
Services: Visits by appointment.
Postal address: Rua Monte Alegre, 984; CEP 05014-901 São Paulo, SP
E-mail address: cedic@pucsp.br

2. Arquidiocese de São Paulo / Comissão de Justiça e Paz de São Paulo *(Archidiocese of São Paulo / São Paulo Justice and Peace Commission)*
Postal address: Av. Higienópolis, 890; CEP 01238-908 São Paulo, SP
E-mail address: antoniocarlosmalheiros@tj.sp.gov.br

3. Grupo Tortura Nunca Mais do Rio de Janeiro (GTNM/RJ) *(Never Again Torture Group of Rio de Janeiro)*
Contents of the archives: Set of dossiers of those killed and disappeared for political reasons since 1964, published jointly with the

Commission of Relatives of Those Killed and Disappeared for Political Reasons and the Institute for the Study of State Violence (IEVE), and the Never Again Torture Group of Pernambuco (cf. Appeniix III, Bibliography).

Postal Address: Rua Maranhão 206; CEP 20720-230 Meier; Rio de Janeiro, RJ

Web Page: www.torturanuncamais-rj.org.br

4. Grupo Tortura Nunca Mais de Pernambuco (GTNM/PE) *(Never Again Torture Group of Pernambuco)*

Contents of the archives: Information on the coup d'état and documents on political assassinations and disappearances. Statements.

Postal address: Estrada do Bongi, 570 (casas 3 e 10); Afogados, CEP 50830-260 Recife, PE

E-mail address: mtnm@torturanuncamais.org.br + amparo@torturanuncamais.org.br

Web page: www.torturanuncamais.org.br

5. Grupo Tortura Nunca Mais de São Paulo (GTNM-SP) *(Never Again Torture Group of São Paulo)*

E-mail address: rosenm@uol.com.br

Web page: www.torturanuncamais-sp.org.br

6. Universidade de São Paulo (USP) / Nùcleo de Estudos da Violência (NEV) *(University of São Paulo / Study Group on Violence)* **Centro de Documentação Especializada** *(Specialized Documentation Centre)*

Contents of the archives: Computerized bibliographical documentation in the form of papers, technical reports, information bulletins, year books and reviews, together with a small collection of books.

Postal address: Av. Prof. Lúcio Martins Rodrigues; Travessa 04 ; Bloco 02; Cidade Universitária; CEP 05508-900 São Paulo, SP

E-mail address: nev@usp.br

Web page: www.nev.usp.br

7. Arquivo do Estado de São Paulo *(São Paulo State Archive)*

Contents of the archives: Historical documents from the dictatorship periods, statements by ex-political prisoners detained in the State Department of Political and Social Order of São Paulo (DOPS). It publishes an Historical Review.

Postal address: Rua Voluntários da Pátria, 596; CEP 02010-000 São Paulo, SP
E-mail address: fausto-arquivoestado@sp.gov.br

8. Centro de Documentação e Memória da Universidade Estadual de São Paulo (UNESP) *(Documentation and Memory Centre of the State University of São Paulo)*

Contents of the archives: Sets of documents (archives and collections of historical value) of information, of reference and of studies and research on contemporary political history, in particular on social movements (workers' movement and parties).

Postal address: Praça da Sé, 108, 1° andar; CEP: 01001-000 São Paulo, SP

9. Coordenadora Ecumênica de Serviço (CESE) *(Ecumenical Coordinating Service Group)*

Object: Ecumenical networking and support to solidarity groups, both local and national, in the field of human rights; publication of information leaflets on the Universal Declaration of Human Rights and the WCC Declaration (cf. Appendix I above)

Postal address: Rua da Graça, 64; Graça, DEP 40150-055 Salvador, Bahia
E-mail address: eliana@cese.org.br

CHILE

1. Fundación de documentación y archivo de la Vicaría de la Solidaridad *(Documentation and Archive Foundation of the Vicariate of Solidarity)*

Contents of the archives: Archive of documents dealing with the social and legal assistance provided by the Vicariate of Solidarity from 1973 until 1992. It contains the major part of the material used by the National Truth and Reconciliation Commission.

Postal address: Erasmo Escala 1884, Santiago
E-mail address: funvisol@iglesia.cl

2. Fundación de Ayuda Social de las Iglesias Cristianas (FASIC) *(Social Assistance Foundation of the Christian Churches)*

Contents of the archives: Archives containing documentation of the various programmes of support to victims from 1975 to the present day: political prisoners, refugees, persons in exile, torture, legal archive (individual trials for disappeared persons, torture, executions and collective trials); councils of war; sentences; testimonies on torture; files on support to victims (approximately 35,000 individuals supported); periodical publications; monographs; press archive; virtual news archive; video archive.

Postal address: Manuel Rodríguez 33, Santiago.

E-mail address: documentacion@fasic.org

3. Corporación de defensa de los derechos del pueblo (CODEPU) *(Corporation for the Defence of People's Rights)*

Contents of the archives: Archive containing documentation of programmes of support to victims (political prisoners, torture victims and exiles) who received assistance in the various institutional programmes of mental health and legal aid, from 1980 to the present day.

Postal address: Bulnes 188. Dpto. 62, Santiago.

E-mail address: info@codepu.cl

4. Agrupación de Familiares de detenidos desaparecidos (AFDD) *(Group of Relatives of the Detained and Disappeared)*

Contents of the archives: History of the Group of Relatives of the Detained and Disappeared, and full documentation concerning cases, legal actions, letters, political pressure campaigns, photographs and videos.

Postal address: Ricardo Cumming 1161, Santiago.

E-mail address: afdd@tie.cl

5. Fundación de protección a la infancia dañada en los estados de emergencia (PIDEE) *(Foundation for the Protection of Children harmed during States of Emergency)*

Contents of the archives: History and documentaion concerning the problems of the repression of children and the effects of human rights violations on minors during the military dictatorship.

Postal address: Holanda 3587, Ñuñoa, Santiago.

E-mail address: pidee@terra.cl

6. Centro de salud mental y derechos humanos (CINTRAS) *(Centre for Mental Health and Human Rights)*

Contents of the archives: Documentation on mental health treatment programmes for victims and documents of theoretical reflection on issues of mental health. Review: 'Reflexión'.

Postal address: María Luisa Santander 545, Providencia, Santiago
E-mail address: cintras@cintras.tie.cl

7. Instituto de Derechos Humanos (Proyecto-ley del gobierno) *(Institute of Human Rights (Proposed Government Legislation))*
At the time of publication government legislation is in preparation to establish an Institute of Human Rights, with the aim of securing the heritage of documentation in the archives (inter alia) of the Vicariate of Solidarity and the Report of the Valech Commission (on the 27,000 cases of detainees and political prisoners and the practice of torture).

PARAGUAY

1. Comité de Iglesias para Ayudas de Emergencias (CIPAE) *(Churches' Committee for Emergency Aid)*
Postal address: Independencia Nacional N°. 579 c/ Azara, Asunción
E-mail address: cipae@cmm.com.py, areadh-cipae@cmm.com.py

2. Centro de Documentación y Archivo para la Defensa de los Derechos Humanos (del Poder Judicial): accesible en la pagina web de UNESCO *(Documentation Centre and Archive for the Defence of Human Rights (of the Legal Authority) : accessible on the UNESCO Web Page)*
Contents of the archives: The 'Archive of Terror' covers two key periods: the one previous to Alfredo Stroessner, covering the 1930s, and the second covering his dictatorship from 1954 until 1989, when Stroessner was defeated. The archive contains extensive information on the Condor Operation of the military dictatorships of Argentina, Chile, Paraguay, Uruguay and Brazil to stamp out opposition. Among the computerized documents there are files on detainees, confidential reports, search warrants, statements on investigations, surveillance of members of the opposition, students and trade-unionists, telephone bugging, lectures, speeches, and various sound recordings..
Postal address: Palacio de Justicia; Mariano Roque Alonso y Pedro Blasco Testanova, 8vo. Piso, Of. 13; Asunción, Paraguay.
E-mail address: ccya@pj.gov.py
Web page (with UNESCO): www.unesco.org/webworld/paraguay

URUGUAY

1. Servicio Paz y Justicia (SERPAJ-Uruguay) *(Peace and Justice Service)*
Contents of the archives: Archive with testimonies, legal proceedings, photos, posters, correspondence, books, reviews, internal material and documentary videos in the 'Luís Pérez Aguirre' Documentation Centre and Library.
Postal address: Joaquín Requena 1642, 11200 Montevideo
E-mail addresses: verdad@serpaj.org.uy; cedoc@serpaj.org.uy
Web page: www.serpaj.org.uy

2. Madres y Familiares de Detenidos Desaparecidos *(Mothers and Relatives of Persons Detained and Disappeared)*
Contents of the archives: Archive of testimonies, posters, correspondence, internal material, maps and documentary videos.
Postal address: Nicaragua 1332 Ap. 205 11800 Montevideo
E-mail address: famidesa@adinet.com.uy
Web page: www.tau.org/familiares

3. Amnistía Internacional – Sección Uruguay *(Amnesty International – Uruguay Section)*
Contents of the archives: Archive of testimonies, posters, photos, correspondence, legal proceedings, internal material and documentary videos.
Postal address: Colonia 871, ap. 5 piso 2, 11200 Montevideo
E-mail addresses: ai_edai@chasque.net / eamen@adinet.com.uy
Web page: www.amnistiauruguay.org.uy

4. Instituto de Estudios Legales y Sociales de Uruguay (IELSUR) *(Legal and Social Studies Institute of Uruguay)*
Contents of the archives: Archive of testimonies, legal proceedings, correspondence and internal material.
Postal address: Plaza Independencia 1376, piso 8, 11100 Montevideo
E-mail address: espanbac@adinet.com.uy
Web page: www.geocities.com/anderspatrik/ielsur.htm

5. Secretaría Internacional de Juristas para la Amnistía en Uruguay (SIJAU) *(International Secretariat of Jurists for Amnesty in Uruguay)*
Archive deposited in the Bibliotèque de Documentation Internationale Contemporaine (BDIC), Université de Paris X, Nanterre, France.
Contents of the archive: The objectives of SIJAU are a general amnesty in Uruguay and the restoration of democratic rights. In the 'Fonds d'Archives sur l'Histoire, mémoire et justice dans le Cône Sud' (Collection of archives on the history, memory and justice in the Southern Cone), there can be found: mission reports, lists of prisoners and disappeared persons in Uruguay, communications with international and regional bodies, studies, publications by Uruguayan political parties and organizations, documents of solidarity, correspondence, manuscripts, dossiers on particular issues, etc..
E-mail address: cecile.tardy@bdic.fr
Web page: www.bdic.fr

II. ANDEAN REGION

BOLIVIA

1. Asamblea Permanente por los Derechos Humanos en Bolivia *(Permanent Assembly for Human Rights in Bolivia)*
Postal address: Avenida 6 de agosto, 548; cajón postal 9282, La Paz
E-mail address: apdhdb@entelnet.bo
Web page: http://web.entelnet.bo/apdhdb

2. Secretaria de la Corte Suprema de Bolivia, en Sucre *(Secretariat of the Supreme Court of Bolivia, in Sucre)*
Postal address: Parque Bolivar, Casillas de Correo 211 y 321, Sucre
E-mail address: cortesuprema@poderjudicial.gov.bo

PERU

1. Coordinadora Nacional de Derechos Humanos *(National Co-ordinating Committee for Human Rights)*
Postal address: Calle Pezet y Monel 2467; Lince, Lima 14

E-mail address: postmaster@dhperu.org
Web page: www.dhperu.org

2. Asociación Pro Derechos Humanos (APRODEH) *(Association for Human Rights)*
Postal address: Jr. Pachacútec 980 – Jesús María – Lima
E-mail address: postmast@aprodeh.org.pe
Web page: www.aprodeh.org.pe

3. Centro de Estudios y Acción para la Paz (CEAPAZ) *(Centre for Study and Action for Peace)*
Postal address: Juan Roberto Acevedo 330, alt. cdra.7 y 8 Av. Sucre – Pueblo Libre – Lima
E-mail address: ceapaz@ceapaz.org

4. Comisión Episcopal de Acción Social (CEAS) *(Episcopal Commission for Social Action)*
Postal address: Av. Salaverry N° 1945 – Jesús María – Lima
E-mail address: ceas@ceas.org.pe

5. Comisión de Derechos Humanos (COMISEDH) *(Commission for Human Rights)*
Postal address: Av. Horacio Urteaga 704 – Jesús María – Lima
E-mail address: comisedh@amauta.rcp.net.pe

6. Fundación Ecuménica para el Desarrollo y la Paz (FEDEPAZ) *(Ecumenical Foundation for Development and Peace)*
Postal address: Jr. Trinidad Morán 286 – Lince – Lima
E-mail address: fedepaz@terra.com.pe

7. Instituto de Defensa Legal (IDL) *(Legal Defence Institute)*
Postal address: Manuel Villavicencio 1191 – Lince – Lima
E-mail address: idl@idl.org.pe
Web page: www.idl.org.pe

8. Mesa Nacional de Desplazamiento y Afectados por Violencia Política (MENADES) *(National Board for Displaced Persons and Persons affected by Political Violence)*
Postal address: Av. Diagonal 550 Of. 401 – Miraflores – Lima
E-mail address: menades@terra.com.pe

9. Asociación Ministerio Diaconal Paz y Esperanza *(Peace and Hope Diaconal Ministry Association)*
Postal address: Jr. Hermilio Valdizán 681 – Jesús María – Lima
E-mail address: aspazes@pazyesperanza.org
Web page: www.pazyesperanza.org

10. Defensoría del Pueblo del Perú *(Defenders of the Peruvian People)*
Contents of the archives: Archives available in Peru on closed circuit in their premises in Lima. Material on human rights in Peru.
Web page: www.ombusdman.gob.pe

III. CONTINENTAL

1. Centro de Documentación del Instituto Interamericano de Derechos Humanos (IIDH) *(Documentation Centre of the Inter-American Institute for Human Rights)*
Contents of the archives: A bibliographical collection on human rights in Latin America: documentation (from 1980 to the present day) describing the experience and knowledge gained in the area of human rights defence, promotion, research and education in Latin America and the Caribbean, related to IIDH's work in education in human rights, the human rights situation, rights of women and children, of indigenous peoples, ombudsman, electoral processes, regime changes, migrants, social and political context, armed conflict and peace campaigning.
Servicios: Access to data base on its web site: htpp://www.iidh.ed.cr/cedoc, specialized annotated bibliographies, web site guides (under specific themes), inter-library loan agreements, lists of bibliographical references, photocopying and scanning of documents and despatch to users worldwide, bibliographical advice on production of academic work.
Postal address: Apartado Postal 10081–1000, San José, Costa Rica
E-mail address: lmolina@iidh.ed.cr, lucreciamolina@corteidh.or.cr, documentación@iidh.ed.cr
Web page: www.iidh.ed.cr/cedoc

2. Federación Latinoamericana de Asociaciones de Familiares de Detenidos-Desaparecidos (FEDEFAM) *(Latin American Federation of Associations of Relatives of Detained and Disappeared Persons)*
Countries with member associations of FEDEFAM: Argentina, Bolivia, Brazil, Colombia, Chile, Ecuador, El Salvador, Guatemala, Honduras, Mexico, Nicaragua, Paraguay, Peru, Uruguay.
Postal address: Fedefam 2444; Carmelitas 1010 – A – Caracas, Venezuela
Office: Edif. Aldomar Piso 7, Of. 55, Marrón a Cují
E-mail address: fedefam@true.net

IV. MERCOSUR REGION AND CHILE

Proyecto Memoria Abierta *(Open Memory Project)*
Contents of the archives: Open memory is a joint activity involving human rights organizations in Argentina, with UNESCO support. A census-guide to human rights archives in the region, making available information from existing sources in the various regional organizations concerned with human rights violations, specifically those perpetrated during periods of state terrorism.The guide brings together information on some thirty archives in organizations in the region, describing their documentary, photographic and oral sources (themes, geographical situation, and time period). Documentation on locations connected with repression and resistance, and locations of monuments and memorials.
Postal address: Memoria Abierta, Av. Corrientes 2560, 2° E (C1046AAQ) Ciudad de Buenos Aires
E-mail address: pvaldez@memoriaabierta.org.ar
Web page: www.memoriaabierta.org.ar